EXPLORIN(

AND ANTIPAXOS

SUSAN VALERIE OMAR BSc FRGS

To my husband Tarek

The author, Susan Valerie Omar has spent two years in Paxos and Corfu and has a great love of Greece. As a professional biologist and naturalist she has written many articles on her travel experiences in the Arctic and Europe, and especially in Greece. She now lives in Dorset with her Egyptian husband Tarek and son Adam.

Published by Römer Designs
Trees, The Ridge
Cold Ash, Newbury, RG16 9HZ

ISBN 0-9516429-0-1

Page set by Gabletek Limited, Great Shefford, Newbury, RG16 7DT

Printed and Distributed in Greece by
SUNSHINE Limited
Ilia Politi 4
Corfu
Greece
Tel. and Fax. 0661 - 36756

CONTENTS

WALKS CONTENTS

/continued

WALKS CONTENTS

INTRODUCTION

A certain indefinable magic bewitches the visitor to Paxos and compels a return visit. What is it that is so captivating about this little island in the Ionian Sea? Maybe it is the unique blend of an enchanting verdant landscape, set in an azure sea, inhabited by some of the world's most charming and hospitable people, and day after day of endless sunshine.

Paxos is said to have been created by the Greek God Poseidon (Ruler of the Seas) as a peaceful retreat for himself and his much loved nereid Amphitriti. With just one mighty blow with his trident, he struck off the southern tip of Corfu, and Paxos emerged from the waves.

The very name Paxos suggests peace (Latin PAX). When children today call a truce in a game of 'chase' they often unwittingly refer to the etymology of the island when they cry 'Pax!'.

Paxos possesses a living symbol of peace and harmony: the olive trees, which cover the whole island like a green cloak, have represented peace since before Noah's dove brought one leaf back to the ark (Genesis 8:1). The 25,000 or so olive trees (Greek ELAYA) on Paxos are as valued today as they were in the mythological past when the goddess Athena first planted olives in Greece near the Athenian Acropolis. Important for its oil, and signifying prosperity and health as well as peace, the olive-bearing tree receives numerous references in mythology and in the Old and New Testaments, eg "His beauty shall be like the olive" (Hosea 14:6). Olive oil, especially fragrant and of high quality in Paxos, is still a major source of income for the islanders.

One of the legendary gods associated with Paxos is the Great Pan, well-known as the goat-like god of all nature (Greek PAN = everything). Legend tells how one day a ship was sailing in Paxos waters when the Egyptian commander Thamous heard a booming voice calling. The voice was coming from the island and it called his name three times. Then the voice instructed Thamous to announce upon his arrival in Corfu that the Great Pan was dead. This supernatural phenomenon is a great legend in Paxos and the death of Pan is linked by some to the death of Christ or, alternatively, to the end of an era of idolatrous gods of Greece (Plutarch, 50-120 AD, describes this).

Christianity was introduced to the island by Saints Gaius and Crispus, disciples of the Apostle Paul. The main town of the island, GAIOS, is named after St Gaius of Derbe who was baptized along with Crispus by Paul himself. "I am thankful that I baptised none of you except Crispus and Gaius" writes the Apostle Paul in 1 Corinthians 1:14, showing his high regard for the two disciples who were his travelling companions while on a 3-month visit to Greece. In the New Testament, St Gaius has several references* and the Apostle John actually addresses a letter (3 John 1) to Gaius with whom he seems to have been well acquainted.

A recently-revived Saint's day dedicated to St Gaius now takes place in midsummer when a colourful assembly of priests of the highest order, and an enormous church band, make a pilgrimage from Corfu for the day.

*New Testament References for Gaius and Crispus: Acts 18:8; Acts 19:29; Acts 20:4; Romans 16:23; 3John 1; 1 Corinthians 1:14.

Panayia Island

Paxos and Antipaxos have preserved a landscape and a way of life which have hardly changed in the last 25 years, and this is due in large measure to the absence of an airport or any developments of hotels. Here you can find a simplicity and a tradition of living that elsewhere in Greece have been swamped by tourism.

As on Corfu, but in contrast to many of the other Greek islands, the population of Paxos is spread over the whole island in hamlets and villages as well as in the three main harbour villages of Gaios, Loggos and Lakka. This creates much of the magic of the landscape which is so intruiging to explore.

Gaios

The main harbour of Paxos and the centre of the island's life, Gaios has a charm unequalled anywhere in the Ionian. The stone flagged waterside square is the hub of the island life: its centre-piece is the dazzling white church flanked by cheerful outdoor café-bars where everyone meets (or waits for) everyone else. Pink and white oleanders add a further dash of colour and the caiiques and yachts moor literally at the edge of the square. The two arms of Gaios Harbour are enclosed by the pine covered isle of St Nicholas with its Venetian castle (now hidden in the trees). From the main square you can catch a ferry, caiique, or express boat to Corfu, Parga, Antipaxos and to Moggonisi Island; and boat excursions around the island start here.

Loggos

Loggos (also spelt 'Longos' and pronounced either way) is a very pretty and unspoilt natural harbour. It lies about 15 minutes by motor boat from Gaios and there is a good beach a couple of minutes walk from the village. There is a telephone office as well as a 'bureau de change' and a number of picturesque waterfront tavernas. Taxis and buses pass through Loggos regularly.

Lakka

Lakka is the most northerly of the three east coast Paxos harbours. The circular bay which is almost completely sheltered from the open sea is excellent for swimming and learning to windsurf. The village is beautiful with a maze of narrow traffic-free lanes flanked with interesting shops and open air tavernas. From Gaios it takes around 40 minutes to reach Lakka by motor boat. There is a telephone and 'bureau de change' and a bus service. At the time of writing, a doctor visits Lakka for a clinic every week.

GEOGRAPHY AND CLIMATE

Position: 39° 10' latitude 20°9' 30" longditude, Ionian sea.
Dimensions: Paxos measures 7 x 2 miles (11.2 x 3.2 km) and Antipaxos 2 1/2 miles x 1 mile (4 x 1.6km).

Distance from southern tip of Corfu: 9 miles (14.4 km)
Distance from Corfu Town by sea: 32 miles (51.2 km)
Distance from Parga (mainland): 11 miles (17.6 km)

Occurance of earth tremors: small tremors which register around 2 on the Richter Scale are recorded every year.

Tides and currents: there are no tides in the Ionian sea but local currents do occur.

Climate

The seven Ionian Islands of which Paxos and Antipaxos count as one, all enjoy predictably long, dry summers with brilliant sunshine and generally calm seas.

Local Winds

The Harbour Master will inform you if high winds are predicted should you intend taking a boat out of the harbour. The sea is generally calm in the mornings and a convection breeze develops late afternoon from the land. The west of the islands are the 'windward sides'.

Topography

Paxos and Antipaxos are of Tertiary, folded, Mesozoic limestone. There is very little surface water as the limestone has been weathered down and eroded into a series of sponge-like hills and cavern-ridden coasts, so most of the drainage is underground. The fine white sands of Antipaxos consist of small, fossiliferous limestone crystals.

The bedrock strata are tilted, sloping down to the east, resulting in a chain of coves and bays on the east with sea-ward sloping rocks, and an almost unbroken line of cliffs on the west coast of both islands. Here there are large sea caverns and the cliffs reach about 590 feet (180 metres). The highest point on Paxos at St Issavros is 813 feet (248 metres), and on Antipaxos 380 feet (116 metres) approximately.

Conversions

Temperature: To convert Celcius (Centigrage) to Fahrenheit, multiply ^{o}C by 1.8 and add 32. To convert Fahrenheit to Centigrade, subtract 32 from ^{o}F and divide by 1.8.

Distance: To convert kilometers to miles, divide kilometers by 8 and multiply by 5. To convert miles to kilometers, divide miles by 5 and multiply by 8.

THE SEASONS ON PAXOS AND ANTIPAXOS

SPRING: March to May (Greek ANEEKSEES) There is a long and indecisive spring period with many false starts to summer weather.	The spring period is especially unpredictable.
SUMMER: June to September (Greek KALOKERRI) Dry and sunny with hot, dry winds. In August thunder-shower rain is common.	The expanded Azores anticyclone to the west sets in by mid-June, this gives the Mediterranean countries fine, dry weather. Dominant winds are hot, dry dusty airstreams from the south (SIROCCO) and from the north (MAESTRO).
AUTUMN: October to November (Greek FTEENOPORRON) Changeable with sunny days interspersed with stormy ones.	An invasion of cold fronts occurs and by 20th October a sudden drop in pressure is accompanied by a marked increase in the incidence of rain.
WINTER: December to February/March (Greek HIMONA) Generally very wet and windy. Occasional frosts but mostly mild.	Sets in quite suddenly. The high rainfall is due to relatively high sea-surface temperatures from October to April. Anti-cyclone is the dominant circulation type.

Seasonal Variations

The table below gives the average day temperature (^{o}C), the number of hours of sunshine and the sea temperature during the period April to October.

APR	MAY	JUN	JUL	AUG	SEP	OCT	
19°	24°	28°	31°	32°	28°	23°	Average midday shade in ^{o}C
7	9	10	12	11	8	7	Number of hours sun daily
16°	18°	21°	23°	24°	23°	21°	Sea temperature in ^{o}C

LIFE ON THE ISLAND

With the swallows arrive the summer visitors to Paxos, and many of the local people are involved in running tavernas and shops and renting out rooms in their houses. Winter is the season for harvesting olives using methods that have hardly changed over the centuries. Almost everyone is 'roped in' for the olive harvest, and it continues to be an important source of income for the islanders. Fishing has always been a profitable occupation for the Paxiots: the sheltered fishing harbours of Lakka, Loggos, Gaios and Spoutzo (and on Antipaxos, Agripitha) provide perfect anchorages. In winter the sea turns dark and many of the boats are taken ashore, where they rest until the milder weather of spring returns, for there is no urgency to harvest the sea. Whereas olives merely rot on the ground if left untended, the fish of the sea thrive.

Many Paxiot households keep poultry and goats on a smallholding basis and some keep bees and make their own feta cheese and wine in addition to their main occupation. Most families have a donkey and there are one or two ponies and a number of mules on the island.

Paxos people are characteristically self-sufficient and will 'turn a hand' to anything, be it their trade or not, as is necessary when living on a small island. They tend to build their own homes, excavate their own water sternas (cisterns) and run their own small businesses with great energy and minimum help from outside the family. Inside the homes evidence of industrious women and girls is everywhere to be seen, including intricately hand-crocheted curtains, tablecloths and mats.

Children learn from an early age to handle motorboats, to help with long hours of fishing and to lend a hand in tavernas. Very often Paxiot children speak more English than their parents do as they are adept at picking up languages. Many also receive special tuition outside school hours at the 'frondisterio' which is a private school (common throughout Greece), for additional tuition. Education is free and compulsory from the age of 6 to 15 and is maintained by State grants. There are Junior schools and a complete (6 class) Grammar school on Paxos: you will notice two of these Neoclassic buildings on the waterfront in Gaios. Children can be educated until the age of 18 in Paxos, after which they may choose to attend college in Corfu or one of six universities in Greece (Athens, Salonica, Patras, Thrace, Ionannina and Crete). All the young men must complete on average 22 months of National Service which they generally commence at the age of 18.

You should not be surprised to see groups of very young children playing in the square after midnight during the summer months: they will have been sleeping in the afternoon and when the temperature drops in the evening it is a welcome respite from the energy-sapping heat of the daytime, and everyone seems to spring into action. In the high season the discos open at 11pm but don't become busy until after midnight, and they remain open until sometimes 4 o'clock in the morning, when the fishermen exchange their 'dancing legs' for 'sea legs' and go directly to their caiiques to land the morning's catch! Thus is the daily tempo of life in a Mediterranean climate.

THE CHURCH

The Greek Orthodox Creed is followed in Paxos, and is the State Religion. The Church of Greece recognises the spiritual primacy of the Ecumenical Patriarch of Constantinople, but is otherwise a self-governing body administered by the Holy Synod under the presidency of the Archbishop of Athens and All Greece. There has in the past been a Bishop of Paxos, but now the diocese has been returned to the Metropolitan of Corfu, whose representative in Paxos is the Episcopal Guardian of Paxos.

Today there are some 64 churches on Paxos and Antipaxos (this works out at a density of one church per 40 head of the population). The handful of resident priests conduct throughout the year wedding and christening services, funerals and custom of the litanies (processioning of the icons) and Sunday worship which vary in locations from week to week, although some churches are used every Sunday.

Priests in Ceremonial Dress on St Gaios Day

Pavement Cafe, Gaios

HOLIDAYS

In addition to the local Saint's Days, the Greek Public Holidays are:

JAN 1st	New Years Day
JAN 6th	Epiphany
MAR 25th	Independence Day
MAY 1st	May Day
AUG 15th	Assumption Day
OCT 28th	'NO! Day' (OCKI! Day) Greece says 'No!' to Italian ultimatum to surrender and enters World War 2
DEC 25th	Christmas Day
DEC 26th	St Stephen's Day

Moveable Holy Days are: Rose Monday
Good Friday
Easter Monday
Whit Monday

The dates of moveable Holy days usually differ from the dates of the same celebrations in the west.

On Paxos August 15th, Assumption Day (Greek PANAYIA = Virgin Mary) is no longer celebrated with a festival in the main square of Gaios. The Day of the Assumption is an Orthodox and Roman Catholic celebration of the taking up into heaven of the Virgin Mary immediately after death. On Paxos 'Panayia' is the day when the gates of the beautiful white monastery of that name on the island of Panayia outside Gaios are opened. Everyone travels across to the monastery to pay homage during the morning.

VISITORS TO PAXOS

Summer is heralded by a colourful array of visitors to Paxos, both of the winged and the human variety. You might see golden orioles and swallows; house martins and bee-eaters; brightly-plumed hoopoes and softly-cooing turtle doves. Other summer-nesting birds and migrants moving north from their winter quarters include black-headed buntings and quail, nightingales and rufous bushcats, and even vultures and eagles are sometimes seen circling at great heights.

Tourism has come gracefully to Paxos: the summer visitors are welcomed and made to feel at home in the friendly and traditional surroundings. The limited number of tourists has brought an additional livelihood to the island, encouraging the young Paxiots to stay rather than to emigrate (as they used to do for the lure of a more interesting life elsewhere). Nowadays the community is exceptionally close: you will often see several generations of one family working together on one concern, be it in a taverna, corner shop or coffee house. Nearly everyone has benefitted from the summer visitors, from the fishermen who sell their catch to restauranteurs, to the shop owners and taxi drivers. Yet the rural charm which is the essence of Paxos is untouched and the island is as lovely as is to be expected of a secret hideaway created by none other than the Greek God Poseidon, who wanted it as an idyllic retreat.

Throughout history Paxos has been receiving an endless procession of visitors from foreign shores. Most of them have been hostile invaders, viewing Paxos as the 'jewel of the Ionian', and one that every power wanted to own. First, from 229 BC until 733 AD it was part of the Roman Empire, and then amalgamated to the Byzantine Empire until 1204 before an occupation by the Normans. Paxos was repeatedly attacked by Corsair pirates during the Middle Ages, which severely disrupted the day-to-day life of the residents: they felt that they would barely have time to put hoe to soil before yet another raid would have to be repelled. No less than 411 years of Venetian rule spanned an era of numerous vicious attacks from the Turks, and the Paxiots stood by their Venetian occupiers in repelling the bloodthirsty sieges which decimated the population.

In 1797 the Ionian Islands were handed to the French democracy for two years, but then a Russo-Turkish siege led to a Septinsular Republic being formed. A second French occupation ensued, the Ionian Islands becoming part of the French Napoleonic Empire until 1814. During this time the British blockaded the island for a long spell and as a direct result many Paxiots died of thirst or starved in a terrible famine. In 1814 the British captured the fort of St Nicholas and in 1817 formed the United State of Ionian Islands under the supreme authority of the British Lord High Commissioner. The islands were under the British protectorate for 50 years. Finally in 1864 the Ionian

Islands were at last amalgamated with Greece. However, there followed the dreadful wars of 1912-23, with the Asia-Minor Catastrophe of 1922, when some one and a half million Greeks living in Turkey were evacuated to Greece. The Italians invaded and briefly occupied both Corfu (Kerkira) and Paxos in 1923, and in 1940 a Greek-Italian war broke out after Greece said "NO!" (OCKI!) to the Italian ultimatum to surrender. The 28th October is still celebrated as 'Ocki!' Day.

However for four years the islands were occupied by the Italo-German forces, until their retreat in 1944 when the British intervened to support the return of the Greek government in exile; but bloody Civil War ensued, lasting until 1949 when the communists were finally defeated. The fate of Paxos and that of the Ionian Islands has followed that of Greece as a whole since this time, with turbulant changes taking place. 1n 1967 the Colonels' Junta overthrew the Government, imposing a dictatorship which lasted until 1974 when an attempt by the Junta to overthrow President Makarios in Cyprus failed. Turkey invaded Cyprus and the Junta collapsed. Shortly afterwards Karamanlis returned from exile to found the New Democracy Party and he promoted Greece's entry into the EEC. In 1981 Greece finally entered the Common Market and the first ever Socialist Government was elected under Prime Minister Andreas Papandreou Leader of the Pan Hellenic Socialist Movement (PAZOK)

At the time of writing (1990) Greek politics is once again in a state of turmoil, no one party having a clear majority.

Thus Paxos people are, and always have been, used to seeing strangers upon their shores. After suffering countless sieges, invasions, occupations and raids at the hands of oppressors and dictators for so many centuries and until such recent years, one must conclude that the Greeks in general and Paxiots in particular are among the most charitable peoples of the earth, for in their language 'stranger' is synonymous with 'guest' (XENY). Certainly every stranger setting foot on Paxos for the first time experiences genuine warmth in the welcome and is indeed made to feel a guest.

Making Friends

ANTIPAXOS HEATHLANDS AND BEACHES.

The Ionian Archipelago is exposed to a number of winds. The local people pay great attention to changes in the direction of the wind and are particularly adept at predicting sudden squalls and rough sea conditions. It is generally calmer in the morning and a breeze develops in the late afternoon. The Harbour Master prefers you to avoid taking a small boat to Antipaxos (and also around the west coast of Paxos) as there are plenty of larger craft which will take you in safety.

You will no doubt have heard that Antipaxos, the sister island of Paxos, has some of the finest beaches in the Ionian. You should not miss an opportunity to discover for yourself the truth of this.

Antipaxos remains much as Paxos must have been before the Venetian olive-planters arrived. The great appeal of Antipaxos, which is only 2 1/2 miles x 1 mile (4 x 1.6 km), lies in its heathlands full of songbirds and butterflies, terraced vinyards, and most of all, the exquisite chalk-blue waters and sandy bays.

Antipaxos has a small resident population augmented by Paxiots who own vineyards and cottages and spend much time here. During the shooting season from August 20th to March 10th, Paxiots flock to Antipaxos to shoot unfortunate migrating turtle doves. This is a time-honoured tradition, perhaps less odd than that of 'fishing' for birds from clifftops (using nets) which took place on Paxos in former times.

The little village of VIGLA in the centre of Antipaxos has a maze of narrow walled paths leading to vineyards and small orchards of fig, lemon and almond trees. You will see pomegranites and quinces ripening in early October: the local people make a sticky jam from these which is eaten using a spoon and taken with a glass of water.

Apart from a spring at KALOYIRI, Antipaxos has little fresh water, and every home has its own sterna for storing rainwater, as on Paxos. The houses are built with limestone blocks which are quarried by hand using a pick and transported with the help of a donkey (Greek YITHAROS). Electricity arrives at Vrika beach by undersea cable from Lionisskari in Paxos which is why you must not drop anchor at either of these beaches.

Antipaxos is an extraordinarily peaceful island and one of the interesting features of it is the way in which the villages are tucked away in the centre. High, painstakingly constructed walls radiate in a network close around, and yet few paths extend to the coast, much of which is inaccessible. The port of Antipaxos is AGRAPITHIA.

Beach at Voutoumi, Antipaxos

GETTING THERE

Many tour operators and travel organisations in western countries provide flights and sea crossings to Paxos in addition to accommodation on the island. You should contact your local travel agent and the Greek National Tourist Organisation for details of how to book.

By Air

Corfu International Airport serves Paxos. Greece's own national airline Olympic Airways and most major western airlines run year-round scheduled services to Athens, and Olympic Airways operates a scheduled forty minute link from Athens to Corfu. Chartered flights direct to Corfu operate from the end of April to October and you should book your flight well in advance, especially if you are contemplating travelling during the peak tourist months of July and August.

On your arrival at Corfu Airport you will need to take a taxi to the port for the ferry. Just say "*sto limani, sas parakalo*" ("to the port please"). The taxi journey takes about ten minutes, and from the port you can take the ferry to Paxos. Several travel agents situated alongside the harbour provide details of departure times and sell the ferry tickets to Paxos.

By Sea

However you travel, the last leg of your journey to Paxos will be by sea. In summer it is possible to reach Paxos by car ferry from Brindisi (Italy); Split and Dubrovnik (Yugoslavia) changing at Corfu; Sivota and Igoumenitsa (mainland Greece); Patras (via bus or train from Athens), and the other Ionian islands, Corfu, Ithaca and Cephalonia.

If you are travelling on an inter-country ferry, be prepared for customs and immigration control at the port of Paxos, even if you joined the ferry within Greece.

Most travel agents throughout the western countries will be able to book your berth on a ferry. If you are taking a car, it is essential that upon arrival in Paxos you confirm with a local shipping agent your return berth to ensure that your car is allocated a space.

By Train Or Bus

The mainland of Greece is connected to the rail network of the rest of Europe. Rail and bus travellers from Athens should enquire from a travel agent for the train or bus which goes to a port on the west coast serving Paxos. Rail passengers will embark at Patras and bus travellers at Igoumenitsa, Patras or Sivota.

By Car

See also under CUSTOMS - arriving by car. Car travellers will arrive in Paxos by car ferry (see above). Travelling by car in Greece is quite possible, yet the majority of visitors hire their transport when they arrive.

Gaios Harbour

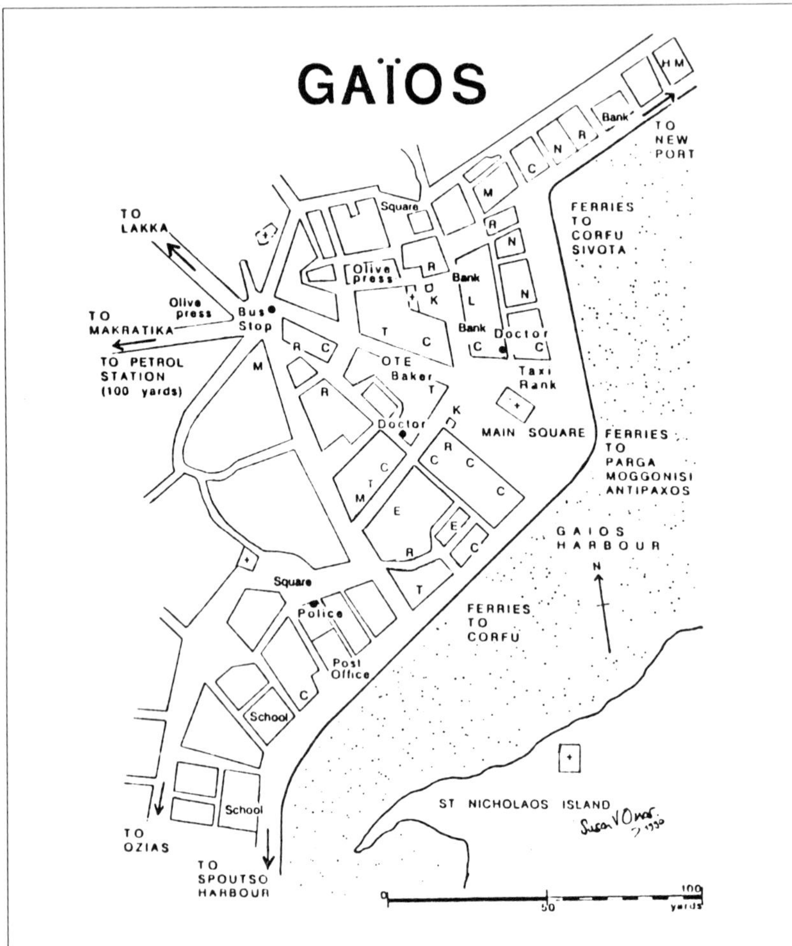

Key

C	=	café-bar
E	=	barber/hairdresser
HM	=	harbour master/port police
K	=	kiosk (newspapers, tobacco) with telephone
L	=	laundry
M	=	minimarket/grocer
N	=	hire of boats and motorcycles
OTE	=	telephone office
R	=	restaurant/taverna
T	=	travel office
+	=	church

PRACTICAL INFORMATION

Information is subject to change.

Accommodation

Outside the peak tourist season (August) accommodation is easy to find in villas and village rooms throughout Paxos. You will find neither high rise blocks of apartments nor luxury hotels on the island as visitors have always been welcomed into the intimacy of the village life here. Self-catering accommodation is ideal for families and it provides the opportunity to enjoy dining out at the numerous tavernas.

If you are travelling independently, numerous travel agents on the island itself will be pleased to organise accommodation facilities for you. Many visitors book package holidays with well-known tour operators from their home countries, and such holidays include the flight to Corfu, the sea crossing and connecting transport as well as self-catering or hotel accommodation. Your local travel agent will advise you. (see "Getting There")

Camping - At present no camping is permitted in Paxos.

Airport

Corfu International Airport serves Paxos, and a ferry connects the two islands. Corfu to Paxos by ferry takes between 90 minutes (Express service) and 3 hours (standard). (See "Getting There")

Banks

Traveller Cheques and Eurocheques can be cashed and foreign notes exchanged for Greek Currency. Credit cards cannot be used for cash: the nearest cashpoint is in Corfu town. There are banks in Gaios and a number of 'bureaux de change' offices also operate in Gaios, Loggos and Lakka.

Beaches and Bathing

On an island only 7 miles by 2, you will never be far from the sea. The west coast of Paxos has a couple of small bays, but mostly cliffs, while the east coast from Lakka in the north to Moggonisi in the south offers a chain of delightful pebbly beaches with safe swimming. Of the 30 or so bays, the majority can be reached most easily by boat. There are sandy beaches at the islet of Moggonisi (reached by express boat from Gaios) and Antipaxos. The beaches of Vrika and Voutoumi in Antipaxos, each with cheerful tavernas, have the finest sand imaginable and the water is an almost unbelievable brilliant turquoise.

Boat Hire

Motorboats and speedboats are available for hire in all three main harbour villages. It is not advisable to take hired motorboats over to Antipaxos or on the west coast of Paxos unless you are specifically told that the boat is suitable for these journeys.

Sailing boats and windsurfers are available for hire in Lakka and at the Paxos Beach Hotel.

Car/Scooter/Motorbike Hire

If you prefer to have some independence, cars can be hired through travel agents on Paxos, and they will be shipped over from Corfu. Cars are useful if you are staying inland (away from the bus route). However, many Paxos beaches are more easily reached by boat, scooter or on foot, than by car.

There are hire centres in Gaios and Lakka for motorbikes, scooters and mopeds.

Minimum age limits are 23 years for car hire, and 16 years for motorbikes, scooters and mopeds.

Currency

The Greek drachma (DRA) has a floating exchange rate.

Import allowed: up to 25,000 Drs in banknotes for a resident of a foreign country. Export allowed: 10,000 Drs plus foreign currencies to a value of US Dollars 1,000. Higher amounts are permitted if declared upon import.

Import of Sterling Travellers' cheques, letters of credit and Eurocheques is unlimited. However these must be in the traveller's name. Foreign banknotes more than US$ 1,000 must be declared at customs upon arrival. Non-compliance will result in fines, confiscation and confinement.

Not endorsed: gold and gold coins unlimited.

The re-export of gold and gold or silver coins is determined by the Credit Sub-Committee.

It is advisable to export Greek Drachma in denominations of 1,000 Drs. as banks in the UK will not normally exchange other denominations.

Note that regulations are subject to change.

Customs

Subject to change, so please check your allowances before travelling.

Visitors aged 18 and over may import into Greece the following items if arriving from the EEC:

1. 300 cigarettes or 75 cigars or 150 cigarillos or 400g tobacco.
2. 1.5 litres alcoholic beverage or 5 litres of wines, sparkling wines orliqueurs.
3. 75 cc of perfume and 3/8 litre eau de cologne.
4. 1000 g coffee or 375 g coffee extract.
5. 200 g tea or 75 g tea extract.
6. Gift articles up to a total value of 55,500 Drs. or, for single gift items a maximum total of 44,500 Drs.

Allowances for travellers returning home vary so it is advisable to inquire at the time.
Note - people under 17 are not entitled to tobacco and drink allowances.
Refer also to 'Currency' for allowances, restrictions etc.

Arriving by Car
Passenger cars can be cleared through Customs for free use for up to 4 months, without payment of import duty or tax. The owner should hold a 'carnet de passage en douanes' issued by the automobile and touring clubs of the country of origin, or alternatively a free use card will be issued by the Customs Authority and an entry will be made in the user's passport.

Arriving by Yacht (flying foreign flags)
For all craft used for pleasure cruising without charging any chartering fee. This category includes self-propelled boats and sailing craft. Upon registration in the owner's passport, craft are entitled to circulate freely for 4 months. Craft with sleeping accommodation are defined as yachts, and these may move freely on the strength of the visa on the Transit Log which is valid for one calendar year. The Transit Log is granted by the Customs and Port Authorities, and may be renewed every year.

Importation of Animal Pets
Cats and dogs require a health certificate from their country of origin testifying that they are healthy and free from any contagious disease and a rabies inoculation certificate issued by a veterinary authority not more than 12 months (cat 6 months) and not less than 6 days prior to arrival.

Visitors from the UK will be unlikely to bring their pets to Paxos in view of their own strict quarantine rules for re-entry.

Importation of Plants
A plant health certificate from the official Plant Protection Service of the country of origin of the plants will be necessary.

Forbidden
The import of plants with soil.

Doctor

There are two surgeries in Gaios. You do not need an appointment and the doctors are always available. The doctors offer a pharmaceutical dispensing service without charging a consulting fee. There is also a clinic in Bogdanatika.

EMERGENCIES: There is a helicopter service to the mainland for medical emergencies.

Electricity

Paxos uses 220/240 AC as in the U.K. but it is advisable to bring continental two pin plugs or adaptors with you if you intend using your own appliances. Electricity was previously generated on Paxos but nowadays an undersea cable connects it to the power network of the rest of Greece.

Embassies

The British Embassy is at 1 Ploutarchou Street, 10675 Athens.

The British Vice Consular Office in Corfu is at 2 Alexandras Avenue, Corfu Town. Tel.0661 30055 or 37995

Consulate General Office of Greece in UK.is at 1A Holland Park, London W12 3TP. Tel. 071 727 8040

Entertainment and Sports

The discoteques, Castello (near the petrol station) and the Phoenix (at the new port) in Gaios, are open every night in the peak holiday season. The discoteque Aloni in Lakka is near the tennis courts. There are tavernas and bars too numerous to mention, not only in the main harbour villages but also inland and on the beaches of Vriki and Voutoumi in Antipaxos. The Paxos cuisine is always fresh and of a high standard: you are guaranteed to enjoy the relaxed and friendly atmosphere of the tavernas where traditional dancing native to Corfu and Paxos takes place in the evenings. You will find that diners linger over their meals in Paxos before going for a midnight stroll (Greek VOLTA) along the waterfront where yachts and motorcruisers add their lights to those of the harbour village, be it Gaios, Loggos or Lakka.

Naturally enough, most sports on the island are centred around sun and sea. WATERSKIING and PARAKITING facilities with tuition are available at Loggos, Lakka and Gaios at the Paxos Beach Hotel. WINDSURFING is fun and you can pick up the skills in a short time in the sheltered conditions of the harbour villages and at Moggonisi. If you are interested in SNORKELING, the coast of Paxos will provide you with a world of undersea caverns and marine life to observe. For the experienced, Paxos Watersport and Diving Club, based in Lakka will take you to the very best locations for SUB AQUA DIVING. You will need to take along your diving certificate together with a medical certificate issued within the past two years. In Lakka you can also play TENNIS on the floodlit courts.

Food and Drink

The Greeks eat very late at night (often finishing their meals at one o'clock in the morning) at the outdoor tavernas with which Paxos is liberally supplied. What could be more pleasant than to enjoy a traditional Greek meal, often to the accompaniment of island music, right at the seafront or under a canopy of vines and passion flowers!

Local dishes include moussaka, pastitsio, souvlaki, spiced chicken, sofrito, stuffed peppers and tomatoes, all with fresh Greek salad (Greek HORRIATIKI) and perhaps beans. Every taverna has a wide variety of fish including sword fish, tuna, kalamarakia (baby squid), octopus, mullet, red snappers and of course lobsters which are in fact crayfish (very expensive as they are becoming rarer). As Paxos has a centuries long connection with Italy you can expect to find Italian dishes on most menus.

Greek coffee is rather special and is served in small cups. It is black, strong and has unfiltered grounds at the bottom. Traditionally it is served sweet together with a glass of water. If you prefer to drink instant coffee with milk, ask for 'Nescafe' and you will be presented with a pot of hot water, a sachet of instant coffee and a portion of milk. Most soft drinks are available as in England: bottled "*limonatha*" and "*portokolatha*" (lemon and orange drinks) are particularly refreshing.

Beers of Greece are of a lager type and very good. Imported beers are available. As with all your purchases, however, remember that the Greek alternative to international brands is always cheaper.

Ouzo is the Greek aperitif tasting of aniseed. It can be taken with water or lemonade, whereupon it takes on a milky appearance.

Koum kouat is the locally made sweet liqueur.

Retsina is wine with pitch-pine or resin added, giving a strong flavour. Antipaxos wine is reputedly the finest in the Ionian and you might have difficulty in persuading a taverna owner to part with a bottle: often demand outstrips supply.

Whether you are looking for breakfast at dawn when the fishing boats are landing their catch; lunch; a snack and drink, or a leisurely dinner, you can always be sure that there is a delightful cafe or taverna not too far away, so "*Kaliorexy*" (good appetite) and "*stin-y-yassas*" (cheers)!

Greek National Tourist Organisation

Corfu: The Governor's House (Diikitirio), Tel. 0661 30060 or 30298
U.K. and Ireland: 4 Conduit Street, LONDON W1R ODJ,
Tel. 071 734 5997.

Handy to have

A Greek phrase book will certainly be useful while staying in Paxos. Although many of the local people understand English and Italian, they always appreciate a visitor who takes the trouble to learn a phrase or two of their language.

Baby food: If you are taking infants and small children with you it is advisable to take with you the milk preparations and baby food to which your child is accustomed as supplies to Paxos fluctuate. Disposable nappies are available in the main shops, together with anything else you might need.

Medicines: It is always advisable to take your own medicines with you as the same products are not always available in Greece. It is a good idea to bring along a first aid kit including dressings for cuts and grazes; sterile wipes; antihistamine cream for insect bites; sunscreen, and medicine for upset stomachs (just in case). If you are unlucky enough to require medical attention, remember that the island doctors are always available. (see DOCTOR)

Health Regulations

No vaccinations or inoculations are required for entry into Greece by persons from the United Kingdom and Europe.

Health Insurance

Visitors from the UK, and other EEC countries are entitled to receive health care in Greece on the same basis as the Greeks. You should apply to your local Social Security Office, well before the date of departure for Greece, for a certificate of entitlement: E111. Fuller cover, however, can be obtained by taking out insurance against all medical expenses, and this you are strongly advised to do. Tour operators and travel agencies can advise you on Travel or Holiday insurance.

Local Excursions

It is certainly worth taking a boat trip around the island to see the picturesque bays of the east coast and then the dramatic limestone cliff walls of the west. Seals sometimes shelter in the numerous sea caverns and a school of friendly dolphins will occasionally escort craft on the short crossing to Antipaxos. Your skipper will probably enjoy an 'ouzo' in the shade while you swim and relax in the tranquil and totally untouched surroundings, before heading back to Paxos.

A day trip by caiique or other craft to Parga on the mainland is most enjoyable. The crossing to the little fishing town takes 75 minutes by caiique or 30 minutes by express boat, and you then have the day to explore this delightful port and to swim from the long sandy bays.

However you decide to spend your time while you are on holiday in Paxos, you are sure to take things at a leisurely pace while absorbing the warmth of the summer sun and the legendary charm of the island.

Petrol Station

There is one petrol station in Paxos which is just outside Gaios. In the months of July and August it is advisable to keep your vehicle well topped up with petrol. Demand often outstrips supply, which comes by boat from the mainland from time to time.

Post Office

Open Monday to Friday. Traveller and Eurocheques can be exchanged here and stamps purchased.

Dolphin

Shops

Generally open from 08.30 to 13.30 and from 18.00 to 21.30. In the peak tourist season shops are closed on Wednesday afternoons and all day Sunday. Outside the peak season early closing is on Monday, Wednesday and Saturday plus all day Sunday.

There are several grocer/minimarkets in Gaios stocking a wide range of products including fresh fruit and vegetables. There are three butchers with fresh and frozen meat and fish, and the town baker supplies fresh crusty bread, croissants and cheese pies.

Gaios has a number of fashion boutiques with swim and leisure wear, and craft shops specialising in ceramic ware, weaving and pottery of traditional style. Quality silver jewellery including copies of ancient Greek designs are particularly outstanding here.

Loggos and Lakka have minimarkets and bakers with a good selection of products in addition to gift shops and general stores. You will also find small minimarkets in some of the small villages throughout the island.

Telephone OTE

OTE is the abbreviation for the Greek Telecommunications Organisation.

Inter-European and intercontinental calls can be made from the OTE offices in Gaios, Loggos and Lakka. Private payphones are also available. You can make telephone calls from kiosks in the main square of Gaios and also from some shops where they have meter phones.

The dialling Code for the UK is 0044 then omit the first zero of the area code.
The area code for Paxos is 0662 and for Corfu is 0661

Time

Greek time is 2 hours ahead of Greenwich Mean Time. In the summer the clocks are advanced a further hour: dates for the change are decided annually.

Tipping.

A good general rule is to give a 10% tip in recognition of good service at restaurants, for taxi journeys, and so on. However you are not obliged to give a tip.

Travel Documents

Passport British citizens require a passport or the simpler British Visitor's Passport. Do note down the main details of your passport so that a substitute document can be issued by the British Vice-Consul in Corfu in the event of loss.

Driving Licence If you intend to hire a car or certain motorbikes you will need to produce a full driving licence. Many car hire companies in Greece will only allow persons over 23 years of age to drive.

Green Card It is advisable, although not compulsory, to take an international insurance certificate if you are driving your own car, and you will need a nationality plate.

Visas Holders of valid passports of the UK do not require visas to travel to Greece for periods of up to 6 months.

Travelling Around

(see also Local Excursions)

INLAND

Taxi
The taxi rank in Gaios is in the main square and the fares are reasonable to anywhere on the island.

Bus
The bus route takes in most of the island's main villages: from Gaios it takes the Makratika route to Bogdanatika and then to Loggos via Fontana and north to Lakka. The bus timetable is displayed in the three harbour villages of Gaios, Loggos and Lakka and changes according to season. The fares are very reasonable and the bus offers a cheerful and convenient means of transport.

Motorbike
If you like to be independent, why not hire a scooter or motorbike if you are 16 or older? Then you can explore the many small tracks to the tiny villages and the coves and beaches along the east coast. (See Car/Scooter/Motorbike Hire).

Car
It is useful to have a car if you are staying inland on the island. (See Car/Scooter/Motorbike Hire)

THE COAST

The west coasts of Paxos and its sister island Antipaxos have spectacular cliffs of limestone with large sea caves. Inside the caves the water appears to be an almost luminous blue as the sun's rays are reflected from the underwater rocks, and thus the caves are known as Blue Grottoes. It is not recommended to take your own boat around the west of the island or to Antipaxos as the sea can become suddenly choppy in the afternoons and there are virtually no bays for shelter. Antipaxos, just one mile to the south of Paxos, has some of the loveliest sandy beaches and the clearest waters in the Mediterranean, certainly not to be missed.

Boat

There can be no more enjoyable way of exploring the coast of Paxos than by taking out a boat of your own. You will discover numerous tiny coves and bays along the east coast where you can swim and sunbathe in totally tranquil surroundings. Don't forget to visit the sandy beach and delightful taverna at Moggonisi in the south as well as the beautiful harbours of Lakka and Loggos. Boats can be hired from these two main harbour villages as well as in Gaios. (See Boat Hire)

Sea taxi /Express Boat

The sea taxi services run throughout the season taking passengers to and from Moggonisi in the south and the beaches at Antipaxos. (See also 'Ferries' below).

Ferries

Special express boats and caiiques operate from the three main harbours of Paxos to take you in safety around the island and to Moggonisi and Antipaxos. Gaios is the main port for Sivota (mainland), Corfu, Ithaca, Cephalonia, Patras in the Ionian and also Italy and connections for Yugoslavia. The Corfu/Sivota ferry makes occasional stops in Lakka and Loggos and there is a caiique service and express boat to Parga. More details and times of departures/arrivals can be obtained from local shipping agents.

Water on Paxos

The high winter rainfall over the Ionian provides water which is stored in the island's specially constructed reservoirs (Greek STERNA). As you explore the villages you will discover beautiful stone reservoirs such as that of Sts. Apostoli in Gaios with a capacity of around 780 cubic yards (600 cubic metres). Some, like the one in Fontana have a hand pump for the locals to draw their fresh water. Most houses inland have their own sternas which are filled with rainwater channelled down gutters from the roof. Sea water is mixed with fresh water in the wells by the sea and this brackish water (Greek GLYPHA) is found in most houses near the coast. The stored water does not last the whole summer and in the past people have suffered severely from lack of fresh water, for there is only a handful of tiny springs on the island. When the sternas run dry water is brought over from the mainland by vehicle at great expense. No one takes fresh water for granted in Paxos and Antipaxos.

Coast near Gaios

View to Avlaki Creek from Agrilas Escarpment, showing water pits in foreground and vineyards on left

EXPLORING PAXOS: THE WALKS

The author has designed 23 walks and rambles to lead you to some of the hidden corners of Paxos of which most visitors are unaware.

On the walks described you will discover windmills and majestic cliffs; short-cut paths through tranquil olive groves to the beaches; ancient olive presses and deserted villages; secret coves and unfrequented bays; old Venetian buildings and churches; caverns and a limestone arch and of course you will have every opportunity to observe the rich diversity of flora and fauna of Paxos and Antipaxos.

With starting points which accommodate visitors staying in different parts of the island, you can choose between short strolls and lengthier trails. It is possible to walk two or three walks end-to-end because the end-point of some walks coincides with the starting points of others: this information is in the text.

Incorporated into the walk descriptions are details of local culture, history and mythology, geomorphology and natural history.

All the walks to **Beaches** and **Inland** are safe and suitable for children. Children should be very closely supervised on any of the **Clifftop** walks.

BEFORE YOU SET OUT:

* For all walks you will need a pair of walking shoes or trainers.
* If you are carrying anything (bottle of water, camera, picnic etc) do put it in a lightweight knapsack on your back to leave both hands free.
* Do take a torch if it is at all possible that you will be walking after sunset: darkness falls very rapidly in these latitudes.
* Do take the latest bus timetable with you.
* Do take something to drink with you.

PLEASE SAFEGUARD PAXOS AND ANTIPAXOS

* The greatest risk to the islands by far is from fire: please stub out all cigarettes with great care and do not light any fires, even on the beach.
* Do not frighten animals or walk through vineyards.
* During the olive harvest, please try to avoid walking over the nets.
* Protect all plants: many of the flowering plants you see on Paxos and Antipaxos are rare elsewhere, so please leave them for others to enjoy.

KEY TO WALKS

Main road
Secondary road/lane
Broad track/walled path
Footpath
Church
Lighthouse
Well or Cistern
Cliff
Olive grove
Cypress trees
Heath/scrubland
Shrine
Spot height
Windmill (disused)
Steps
Lookout point
Anchorage
Sand / pebbles.

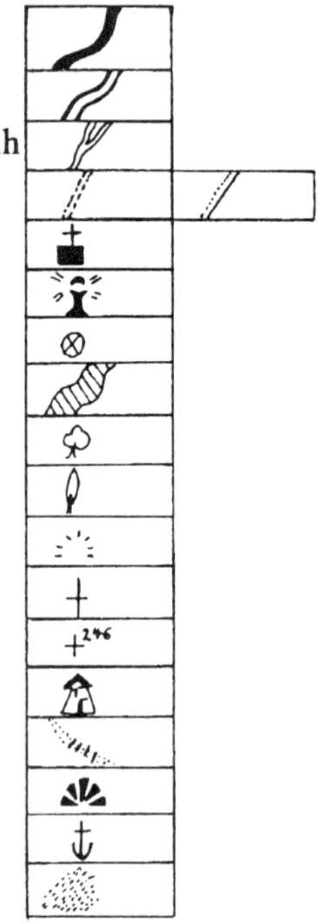

Footpath walled on one side

NOTE: The following maps each show in detail only the walks described. For an overall picture of Paxos and Antipaxos footpaths please refer to the general map also drawn by the author.

Conversion:

Kilometres:	0.8,	1.6,	3.2,	4.8,	8,	16,	80,	160
Miles:	1/2,	1,	2,	3,	5,	10,	50,	100

32 yards = 35 metres

All references to distances are approximate and are quoted in both miles and kilometres.

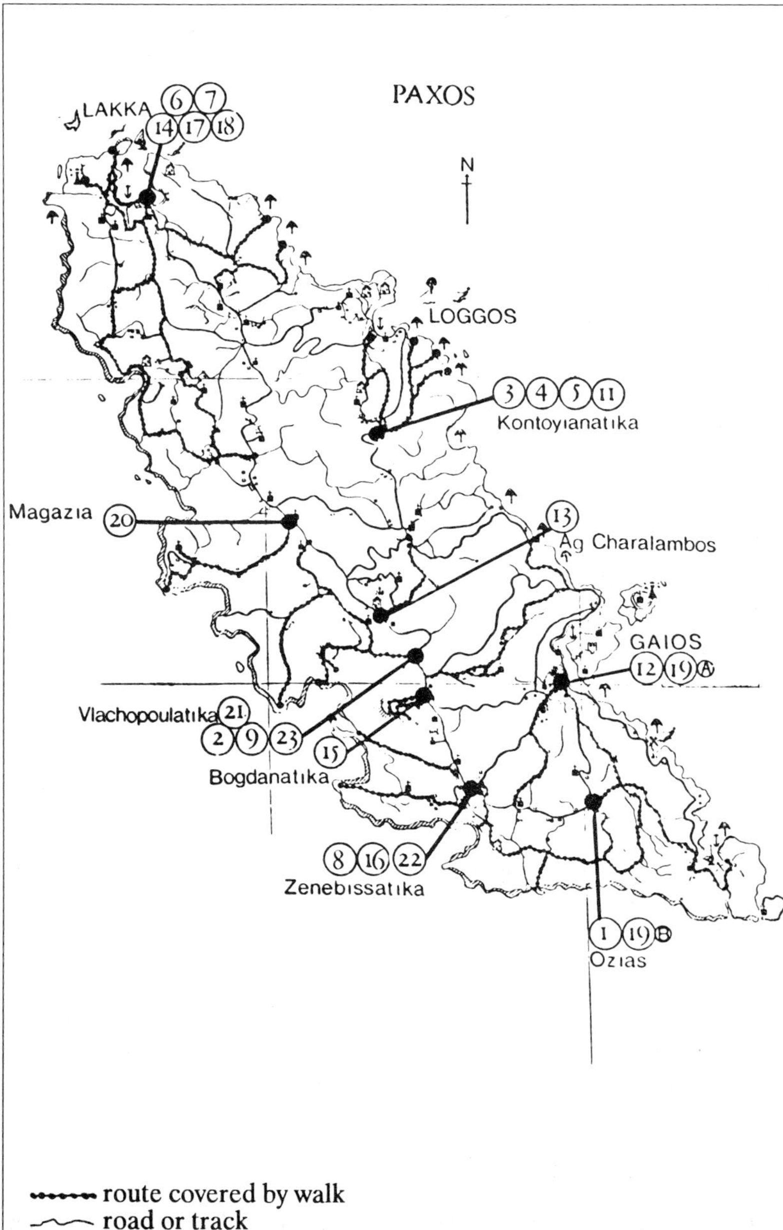

PAXOS WALKS
Starting Points and Routes to Numbered Walks

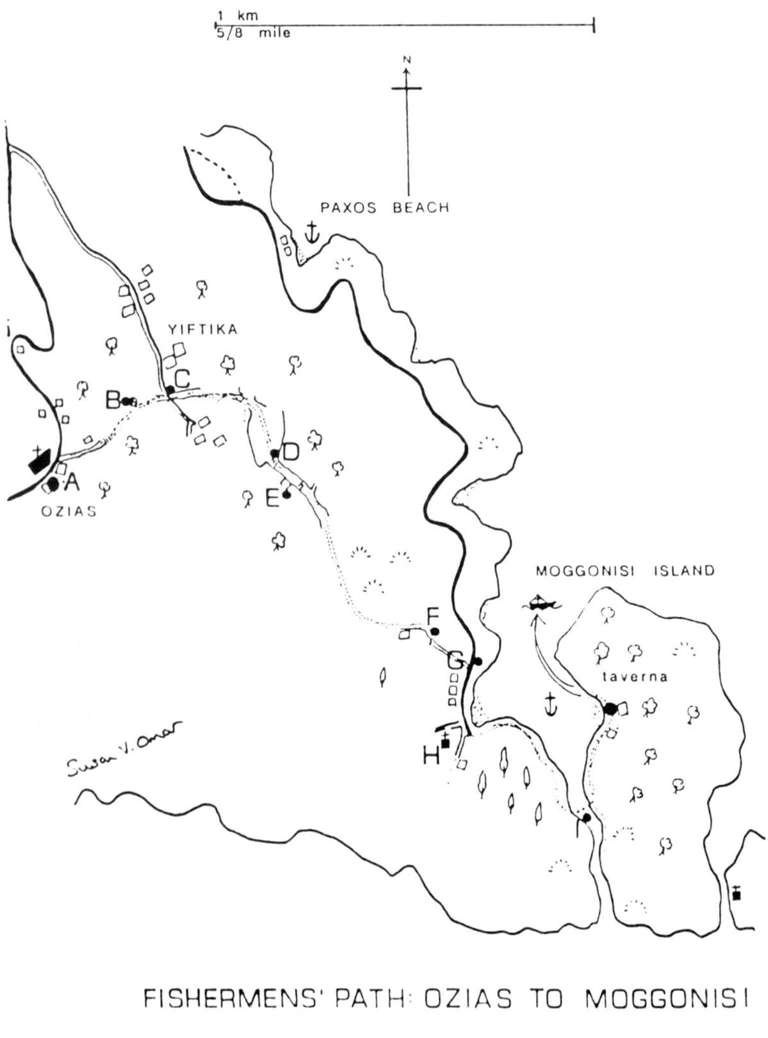

FISHERMENS' PATH: OZIAS TO MOGGONISI

1. THE FISHERMAN'S PATH: OZIAS TO MOGGONISI 1 1/2 miles (2.4 km)

An easy walk for all the family through olive groves to the sandy beach on Moggonisi Island.

Beach facilities: taverna; wind surfing; and an express boat service runs regularly to Gaios (6 mins) and Antipaxos (8 mins) in the high season.

From the same starting point as walk 12.

STARTING POINT: **Ozias café.**

Ozias is reached by either of two roads from Gaios or by footpath through olive groves (walk 12). You may also join the walk nearer Gaios at YIFTIKA (see below).

A CAFENEION is traditionally a place where men gather to drink coffee (Greek KA-FAI), play cards and while away the hours, exchanging local news and views. Greek coffee comes in small cups and is very strong, the grounds being unfiltered. The sugar is added before boiling and you should specify whether you would like SKETO (without sugar); METRIO (medium) or GLEEKO (sweet). The Ozias Cafeneion is a favourite watering hole for many of the local fishermen.

Standing in the lane with the cafe on your right and the church of St Paraskevi on your left, you will see a low pink building adjacent to the café **[A]. The track begins on the left side** of this building. It leads downhill as a walled footpath amongst olive trees. At the bottom of the slope there is a deep, stone-lined fresh-water well (Greek PIGARTHI) on the left **[B]. Follow the path across a dry watercourse and uphill to a lane [C].**

OPTION : For Gaios (3/4 mile or 1.2 km) and the 'gipsy village' of Yiftika turn left at C.

OPTION : For Walk 19 to Tripitos Arch, turn right at C.

Cross directly over the lane to join a walled track which goes slightly uphill, bearing to the right. As you continue between crumbling dry-stone walls you may see a small flock of sheep roaming amongst the olives, their bells clinking. The trail winds through shady olive groves before emerging into a peaceful grassy glade. **The walled track resumes at the far end of the glade [D]** with a few stone steps upwards. You pass a derelict building **[E]**. In the meadow on the right you may see many butterflies (Greek PETAL-OUTHA) flitting in the sunshine. At the brow of the hill the mainland mountains eastward come into view. On the sunny limestone walls up to five different species of lichen grow all within a radius of one metre. Lichens grow very slowly radially (only a fraction of an inch a year) and it is possible to put an age to them simply by measuring the diameter of growth. Thus one can estimate the minimum age of the wall upon which they grow: in this case the walls date back to the first arrival of the Venetians in 1386. The presence of lichens is indicative of an unpoluted atmosphere, and here you can pick out different species by their colours, ranging from pale pink, black and olive grey to white and orange.

Some of the rocks here, when struck, give off a characteristic 'bad egg' smell of sulphur dioxide as you are nearing the Ozias sulphur springs which are centred at the bay of LIONISSKARI below you. A daily swim in the waters there is said by the Paxiots to prolong life.

The path continues over heathland and then winds downhill, becoming narrow amongst myrtle bushes. A wall and house is on your right and a wire fence on the left. **You reach a concrete track [F]** which leads **directly downhill** to the coast road **[G]** and you have a wonderful view of olive-clad Moggonisi Island across the sheltered Ozias harbour known as Spoutso. Antipaxos is visible between the two islands of Paxos and Moggonisi. **Turn right at the coastal lane**, passing the ruined 6th Century St Marina Church **[H]**. The St Marina well here supplies brackish water (Greek GLYPHA). The lane ends and a **waterside track continues round the bay to a causeway [I]** which connects the islands. Depending upon recent weather conditions, you may or may not have to paddle across the 25 yard gap. Follow the creek to the right for a better view of Antipaxos from the windswept cliffs, riddled with cracks and crevices. In the evenings you will see caiiques and small fishing boats quietly chug-chugging southwards to Antipaxos to lay their nets for the night's catch. The nets are collected at daybreak and if you are up early you will see the catch being brought in at the quayside of Gaios and sold on two adjacent stone tables in the square (Greek PLATEEA).

<u>TO RETURN</u>: To Gaios by coastal road 2 miles (3.6 km); **by express boat (7 mins) OR** if you return the way described above, turn **RIGHT at the Yiftaka lane** for Gaios - 2 miles (3.2 km).

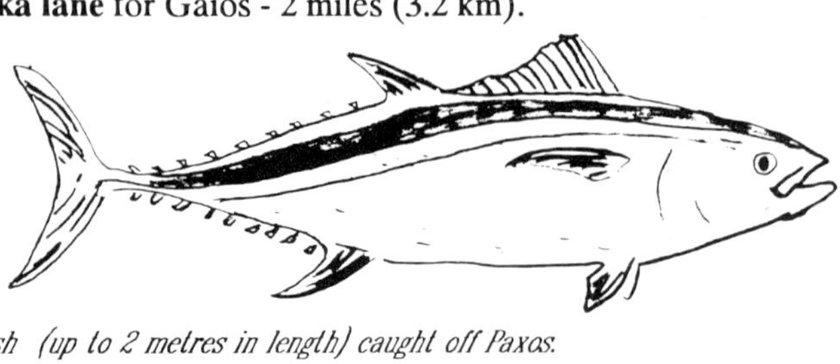

Tuna Fish (up to 2 metres in length) caught off Paxos.

2. TO KLONI-GOULI via the DESERTED VILLAGE. 1 3/4 miles (2.8 km)

This is an interesting downhill walk along broad tracks, exploring the hidden and deserted village of GERAMONACHOS and reaching the pebble beach at Kloni-Gouli at the foot of the cypress-clad hill. (Kloni-Gouli is 1 1/4 miles (2 km) by coastal road from Gaios, a suggested return route.)

From same starting point as walks 21 and 23.

<u>STARTING POINT</u>: The Vlachopoulatika Road junction at Bogdanatika [A]. If you are travelling by bus ask for *"Vlackoplaticka, sas parakalo"*. **Facing south on the main road**, the bus stop, taverna and side lane to Vlachopoulatika are on your right and the **road to the New Port branches off the main road ahead of you** to the left. **Take this road**, which is signposted 'NEO ΛIMANI - NEW PORT' **and after 20 yards take the first lane on the right [B]. Turn to the left at a branch** in the lane by a new house and two old limestone kilns (which now house domestic animals) **[C]**. The lane continues amongst spaced out olive trees which astonishingly manage to glean nutrients from the spartan soil within crevasses in the limestone bedrock.

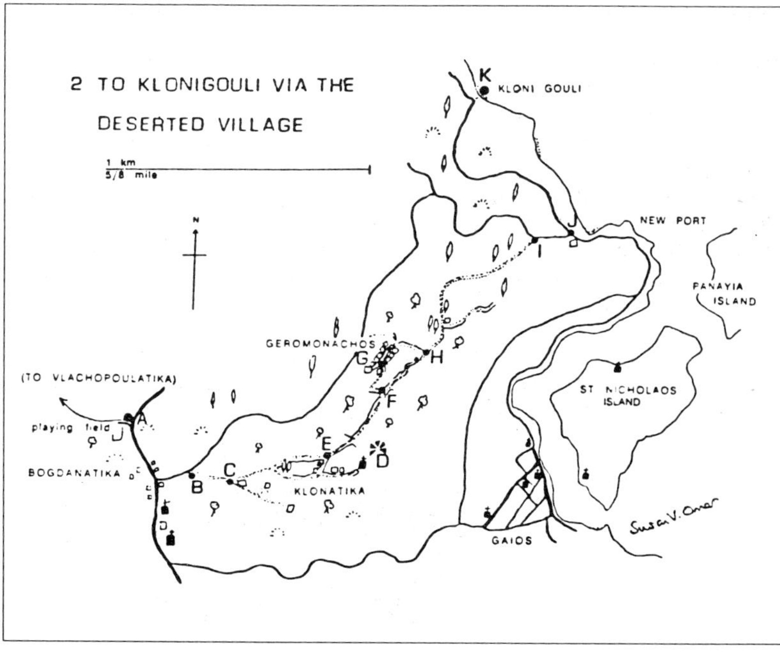

You reach another fork by a clump of cypress trees. **Turn to the right** for a diversion to the hilltop hamlet of KLONATIKA and, beyond the hamlet, the fine church of St Ioannis **[D]**. This is a most peaceful spot with views over Paxos to Antipaxos. **Return to the hamlet and turn right between two houses** to follow a narrow walled path which rejoins the main track. **Turn right [E]**. You pass a red metal gate on your right and reach a quiet limestone plateau with scattered olives. **Take a walled path on the left** which begins alongside a high fenced area (with a notice 'Oil Drilling Possible Danger') **[F]**. This fence is on your right as you follow the path which becomes less distinct. **Turn right and downhill** amongst the trees and within a couple of minutes **you join a walled path and the deserted village [G]**.

Every step takes you back through the centuries in this rural landscape. The very olive trees around you were planted in Venetian times, and the melodious tinkling of the sheep bells contrasts with the uncanny silence of the gloomy forsaken village. A group of stone buildings in dense shade are all that remains of a once thriving hamlet: the houses of Geramonachos are mostly in ruins and include four olive presses, two open sternas and a cluster of dwellings. Wander through the village enjoying the pleasant aroma of wild herbs. **With the downhill slope on your left** you will come to a **white shrine at a T-junction in the path. Turn right and follow the broad shady ride uphill. You rejoin the main track** once again and **turn left [H]** The ride leads downhill in most attractive surroundings with views of Moggonisi Island in the south over terraced hillsides. **Keep straight ahead at a junction** by a house and the downhill track that you are on becomes a cypress-lined lane. After a few minutes **you will reach the road from the New Port (right) to Bogdanatika (left, uphill) [I]** and a view of the sea and mainland. **Bear right (downhill)** and opposite a new villa on the right ('Villa Varvara') **follow a road leading downhill to the left [J]**. From this point it is 3/4 mile (1.2 km) right to Gaios and 1/3 mile (0.5 km) downhill to the attractive beaches **[K]**. There is no shade at mid-day so be careful not to get too hot. The road leads to the coast where there is a string of small bays ideal for swimming and snorkeling.

TO RETURN: To Gaios: Follow the coast road via the New Port: just over 1 mile (1.6 km).

TO RETURN: To Fontana: Continue along the beach road : 1 mile (1.6 km) uphill.

TO RETURN : To Bogdanatika: 2 miles (3.2 km) uphill by road.

3 & 4 WOODLAND WALKS TO (3) LOGGOS BEACH AND (4) MARMARI BEACH 3/4 mile (1.2 km) each

To emerge from tranquil olive groves onto a beautiful beach with crystal clear waters is an experience you will not forget. These two easy downhill walks are exceptionally beautiful. The more northerly bay, Levrechie, has paragliding and water skiing facilities as well as refreshments. Loggos village with its waterfront tavernas and bus connection to the rest of the island is just around the corner from the beach. The two beaches are less than a mile apart by path.

From the same starting point as walks 11 and 5

STARTING POINT: by bus you will alight after Fontana en route to Loggos from Gaios **[A]**. Ask for *"Kontogyinatika, sas parakalo"*. As you approach Loggos from Fontana, **look for a white church and broad stony track on the right at the sharp lefthand downhill bend**. The bus normally stops 30 yards beyond this opposite an olive press. **Begin at the broad track and follow it** through a flat grassy region with olive trees growing at intervals. **Continue ahead at a cross-paths, passing a shrine on your right [B]**. The path bears left. At a new villa ('Chrissa') the track turns sharply downhill to the right. Look out for two concrete gateposts bordering the lane. **Your path leads downhill to the left immediately before the gateposts [C]**. There are intermittent stone steps as you follow the path downhill through a most beautiful region of myrtle (Greek MYRTIA) and tall cypress trees. To your right you will glimpse the bay at Marmari. Reaching some terraced groves **the path forks just after some more downhill steps. Turn right with a low wall on your left**. The path then bears left and **you arrive at a house ('Villa Marmari') [M].**

WALK 3. TO LOGGOS BEACH (LEVRECHIO):

Keep straight ahead with Villa Marmari on your right. The walled path goes down several stone steps and suddenly you can see the bay. You are at the floor of an olive vale and can **follow the dry watercourse or either of the two paths directly to the beach [3].**

TO RETURN: **The village of Loggos is reached by concrete track at the north end of the beach**. The road, village and bus stop are just around the headland (4 minutes walk).

WALK 4. TO MARMARI BEACH:

Turn right with the house on your left. The stony path leads through an olive valley directly to the tranquil bay **[4]**. Marmari Bay is protected by low rocky headlands at each end and shady olives grow literally to the edge of the pebble beach, making a secluded haven for songbirds and sunbathers alike.

TO RETURN: Follow the path back to Villa Marmari and turn right for Loggos Beach and Loggos.

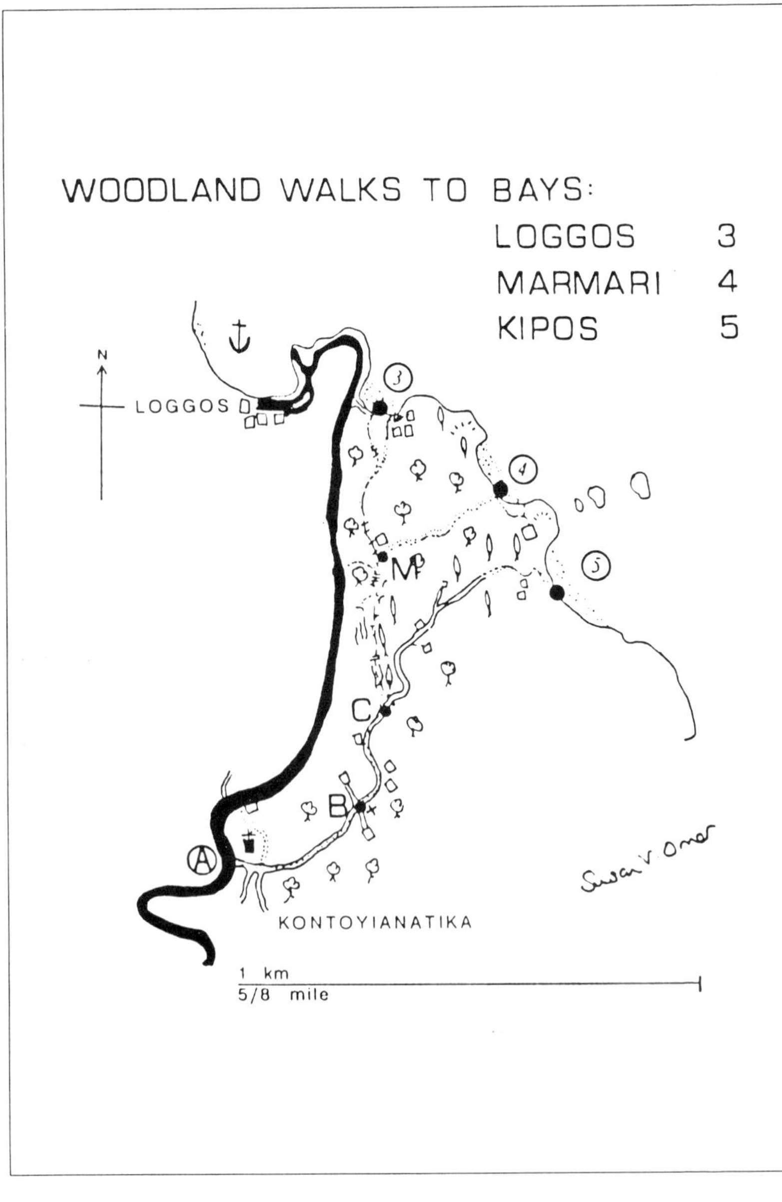

5. KIPOS BAY FROM KONTOYIANATIKA 3/4 mile (1.2 km)

The beautiful beach at Kipos is situated at the foot of an olive-covered hillside. It is a most relaxing and serene location. The walk is along an unmetalled lane.

From the same starting point as walks 3, 4 and 11.

STARTING POINT: By bus you will alight after Fontana en route to Loggos from Gaios. Ask for "*Kontogyinatika, sas parakalo*". As you approach Loggos from Fontana, look for a **white church and broad stony track on the right at the point of a sharp lefthand downhill bend [A]**. The bus normally stops just beyond this next to an olive press. **Begin at the broad track and** follow it through a flat grassy region with olive trees growing at intervals. **Continue ahead at a cross-paths,** passing a shrine on the right **[B]**. The path bears left. At a new villa ('Chrissa') the track turns sharply downhill to the right. **Walks 3 and 4 to Loggos and Marmari Beaches branch off from here [C]**. It is now only a five minute walk to Kipos. You continue downhill and there are views of the sea to the left. **Bear right at a junction** (the left fork is blind ending) and you will be among aromatic cypress trees. For a section the track is fenced at either side among heather and myrtle, and suddenly you are on a low rise above the beach **[5]**. **There is a twisting path leading to the northern corner of the beach** and you can see Panayia Island with its monastery and lighthouse to the south. At the north of the bay are the rocks which outcrop in the sea: a hazard to fishing boats and ferries calling in at Loggos.

TO RETURN: To Loggos via starting point and by road: 1 1/2 miles (2.4 km).

To Loggos via the Millers Path to Koutsi Windmill (walk 11): 1 1/3 miles (2 km).

To Loggos via Loggos Beach (walk 3): 1 mile (1.6 km).

6. FOREST PATH TO OROKOS BEACH 1 1/8 miles (1.8 km)

The walk to Orokos Beach (outside Lakka on the east) is almost as charming as the bay itself. Few visitors are aware that this lovely little beach can be reached by a footpath which leads along an enchanting wooded valley. Once you have discovered this route you will certainly return many times.

This easy route is ideal for those staying in Lakka or in the surrounding hillsides. The beautiful pebble beach offers shade, safe swimming and views of Corfu and Epirus.

From same starting point as walks 7, 17 and 18

STARTING POINT: **Lakka waterfront: the slipway [A]**

This is the local stage for the daily drama of the arrival of ferries and supply boats. Nearly everyone turns out, either meeting friends and visitors to the island, or collecting their packages from Corfu which will be anything from potted plants and spare wheels to trays of cakes and tins of paint.

Before setting off for your walk, don't forget to buy some provisions for you may want to linger for the whole day at the beach.

Setting out from Lakka, join the main bus route south, passing the Lakka Aquarium on the left **[B]. Follow the road uphill for 1/4 mile (0.4 km).** On an uphill lefthand bend **you pass a track on the left. Take the next track on the left just a little further on** by a row of the island's tallest columnar cypress trees (Greek KIPAREESI) **[C]. Keep to the main broad stony track for nearly 1/2 mile (0.8 km)** until it becomes walled and **you reach a T-junction [D]**. Orokos is 3/8 mile (0.6 km) from here.

OPTION : Turn right for walk to LAKKOS BEACH (1/2 mile, 0.8km), - see walk 7.

At the T-junction is a sign on an olive tree (to some cottages and a large old stone building). **Your path starts obscurely to the right of this building.** You have to **leave the stone track and venture into the olive grove behind the building. Pass an open sterna [E] and you will join the faint footpath** (Greek THROMAKOS) which twists and turns downhill **to a dry watercourse at the foot of the hill**. This is marked by a group of dark cypress trees. Once you have reached the watercourse you have picked up the faint thread of the path which soon becomes distinct. It is a most attractive walk frequented by local people. **The path follows a deep narrow valley through the trees with the**

watercourse on the right, and then, in a heathery glade, it merges into the stream bed. It soon emerges on the right bank, among myrtle (Greek MYRTIA) bushes. There is a somehow primeval atmosphere to the deep lush valley: the contorted olive trees close out the sky, filtering the sunlight to an ethereal green.

The path continues through myrtle and then through sunny glades of heather and young cypress trees before running alongside a fence to the left **[F]**. Here there are a number of round stone houses. **Finally you emerge at the olive-lined beach.**

<u>**TO RETURN**</u>: by same route.

6 FOREST PATH TO OROKOS BEACH

7. LAKKOS BEACH FROM (i) LAKKA & (ii) ARGYRATIKA
1 1/4 miles (2km) & 1 mile (1.6 km) respectively

The small pebbly beach at Lakkos (on the north east coast), set against a backdrop of cypress trees, can easily be reached via an attractive walk along a broad track. The water is clear and snorkeling is superb.

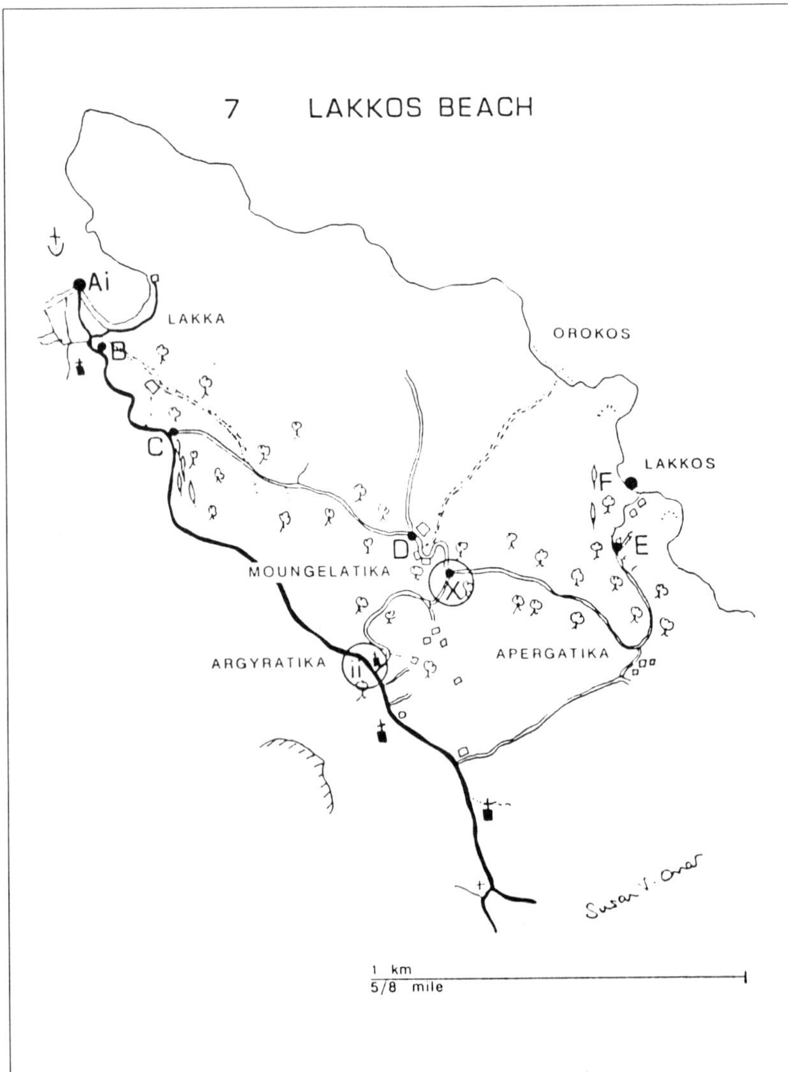

From same starting point as walks 6, 17 and 18

STARTING POINT:
(i) The quayside, Lakka [A]
(ii) The bus stop at Argyratika on the main road (ii). The track begins by a stone church which is on the right as you face towards Lakka, a little further on from the bus stop (going towards Lakka).

(i) From Lakka quayside **[A] follow the main bus route south** passing the church on your right and Lakka aquarium on the left **[B]. After 1/4 mile (0.4 km) walking uphill take the second broad track on your left** just after a lefthand bend **[C]**. Continue along the track for nearly 1/2 mile (0.8 km) until **you reach a T-junction** with an old stone building ahead **[D]**.

OPTION : Forest walk to Orokos Beach (walk 6) branches from here. **Turn right for Lakkos. After 3/8 mile (0.6 km) the road leads uphill and reaches a fork:** uphill to the right and downhill to the left. (Route (ii) joins here from the right). **Turn left downhill. [X]**

OPTION: Back to the road and bus stop, turn right here (1/4 mile, 0.4 km).

(ii) From Argyratika. **Join the track behind the attractive stone church and keep to the main lane**, ignoring two side turnings to the hamlet of Argyratika to the right **after 3/8 mile (0.6km) a track joins from the left** (this is the path described in route i). **Keep ahead [X].**

(i) and (ii) continue from [X]
Continue downhill. You will have glimpses of the bright blue sea (Greek THALASSA) sparkling invitingly through the shady olives. The only sounds to disturb the tranquility will be the lapping of gentle waves on the shore. Near the bottom of the hill are three side turnings to the right and **a house at a T-junction [E]. Turn left downhill** for the beach **[F]**. The path becomes stony and leads through mature scrubland (Greek HAMMOKLATHA) to an olive and cypress valley. You pass two villas and after a final downhill section **reach the remote and beautiful beach.**

TO RETURN: To Lakka via route (i), turn right at [X] (1 1/4 miles, 2 km). Via Argyratika village (route ii), keep ahead at [X] (1 mile, 1.6 km).

8 VALLEY TRAIL TO AVLAKI CREEK

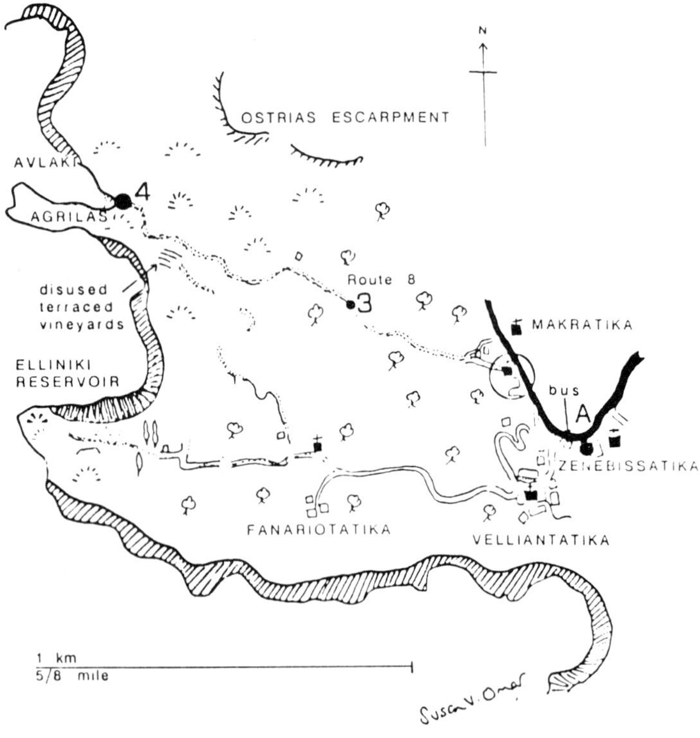

8. VALLEY TRAIL TO AVLAKI CREEK 3/4 mile (1.2 km)

There are very few beaches on the west coast of Paxos as it is mostly cliffed. The picturesque and sheltered creek of Avlaki is especially pleasant for sunlovers in spring and late autumn as it catches every last ray of sunshine before the sun sets over the sea. You should wear trousers to protect your legs from scratches from prickly shrubs.

From the same starting point as walks 16 and 22.

STARTING POINT: **The bus stop at Zenebissatika, 1 mile (1.6 km) outside of Gaios [A].**

Upon alighting from your bus at a bend in the road by a taverna, **walk along the road uphill for about 80 yards**, passing on the left the turning to Velliantatika. **You will reach a bell tower or campanile on your left** opposite some cottages. **The walk begins under the arch of the bell tower [2].**

You join a track which leads downhill along an olive valley where local children often play football and table-tennis among the trees. Lush bracken grows high here in summer and you will see tethered or hobbled goats with their kids. In spring when the little white kids are very frisky and young, they caper about in the bracken like miniature gazelles.

The trail leads northwest along the valley floor, crossing a watercourse and veering to the right of the valley [3]. Above you to the right is the impressive Ostrias limestone escarpment (walk 15). The path emerges from the shady olive groves into heathland (Greek REEKIA) and now **crosses onto the left bank of the gulley.** Rounding a flank of the hillside you suddenly see the sea ahead, together with sheer cliffs and the little creek of Avlaki. **The path leads to the stony creek** (Greek KOLPISKOS) **[4]** through some rather prickly scrub, passing an old vineyard terrace to the left. The headland at Fanariotatika (walk 22) is above you on the left. At the bay you can swim in the sheltered waters or explore the little headland.

TO RETURN: by same route.

9. PIRATES COVE 1 mile (1.6 km)

The pleasant walk to Vlachopoulatika is followed by a stunning clifftop donkey trail to an almost unknown sandy creek. The rather steep final descent should not be tackled without good walking shoes. The vegetation is prickly in places.

From same starting point as walks 2 and 21.

STARTING POINT: **Vlachopoulatika bus stop [A]**. The turning for Vlachopoulatika is on the left as you travel from Gaios to Magazia on the main bus route, 1 1/4 miles (2 km)from Gaios. Ask for "*Vlackoplatika, sas parakalo*" on the bus. The bus stop is by a friendly taverna.

Follow the old road to Vlachopoulatika past the Paxos football pitch on the left [B]. Paxos Football team regularly travels 'overseas' (to Corfu) with a boatload of supporters for 'away matches' in the winter. **Continue for 1/2 mile (0.8 km), ignoring side lanes**, until you reach the village and a little square **[C]**. The lane continues, veering to the left and leads to a cluster of traditional Paxiot houses with colourful gardens. **At the end of the lane [D]** a walled path leads to the left (walk 21) and one to the right. **Turn right. A path follows the contours of the hillside** through an olive grove, the hill sloping away to your right. **The track emerges in open heathland** (Greek REEKIA) at the hilltop near a cliff edge, **and then begins to zig-zag down**. You pass very near to a precipice on your left **[E]** and from this overhanging rock the cliffs drop hundreds of feet to the sea below you where a huge sea cavern can just be seen. You have a breathtaking view south of sheer cliffs at the bays of Prasses and Neradou and Agrilas Headland guarding Avlaki creek (reached by walk 8). Now looking northwest you will see the headland at Ortholithos (see walk 23) and **at the foot of the hill is a tiny sandy cove [F]**. This beautiful little creek at the head of a deep wooded gulley can be seen from very few points from land and sea and when you reach it you almost expect the notorious Corsair pirates of the Middle ages to appear out of the cypress trees! These medieval pirates who infested the Mediterranean were mostly Moors operating from Algiers, Tunis and Tripoli. Paxos had a tradition of repelling all invaders with great bravery: pirates were habitually tossed over clifftops.

9 PIRATES' COVE

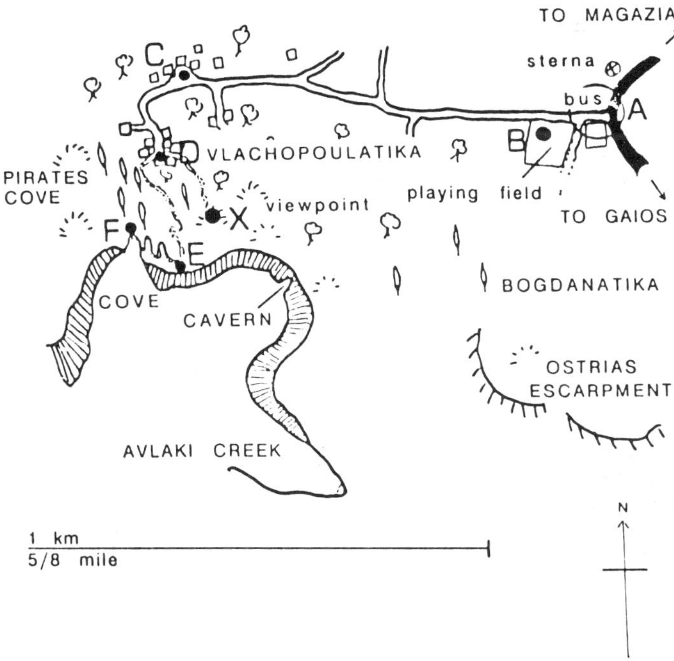

The stony path wends its way down to this creek over open heathland. Sheltering in the heather (Greek REEKI) you may be startled by partridges (Greek PERTHIKA) which will 'freeze' motionless almost until you unwittingly step on them! **Try to note your downhill route as it is easy to miss the path on the way back and to end up in an inpenetrable thicket of cypress.**

<u>**TO RETURN**</u>: You can make your way back **to the bus stop** to enjoy some refreshments at the taverna while waiting for your bus.

10. ANTIPAXOS ROUND TRIP **1 mile (1.6 km)**

GETTING TO ANTIPAXOS

From the harbours of **Lakka** and **Loggos** are **boat connections to Antipaxos.**

From Gaios run the excellent **express boats and caiiques to Vrika and Voutoumi beaches:** they will often take you there via the Kaltsionisi channel to visit a 'blue grotto' (sea cave of remarkable hues) at TSOUHO. On the journey over, fish are frequently seen jumping or "flying" over the surface of the water as they propel themselves out of the reach of the hungry jaws of predator fish.

Make sure to check for your return journey the time and place your boat leaves.

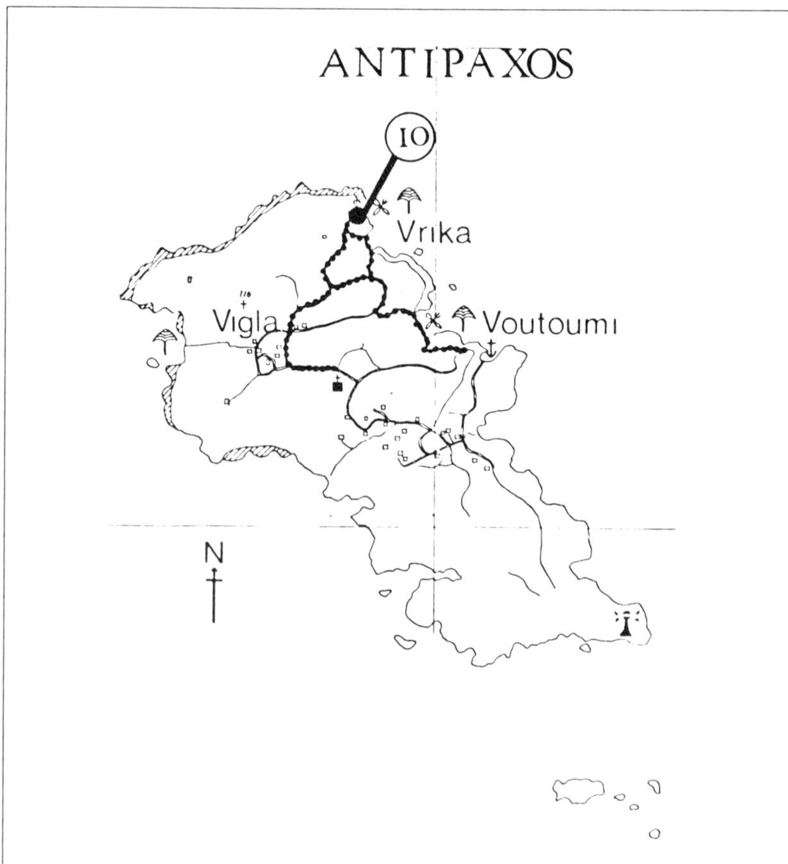

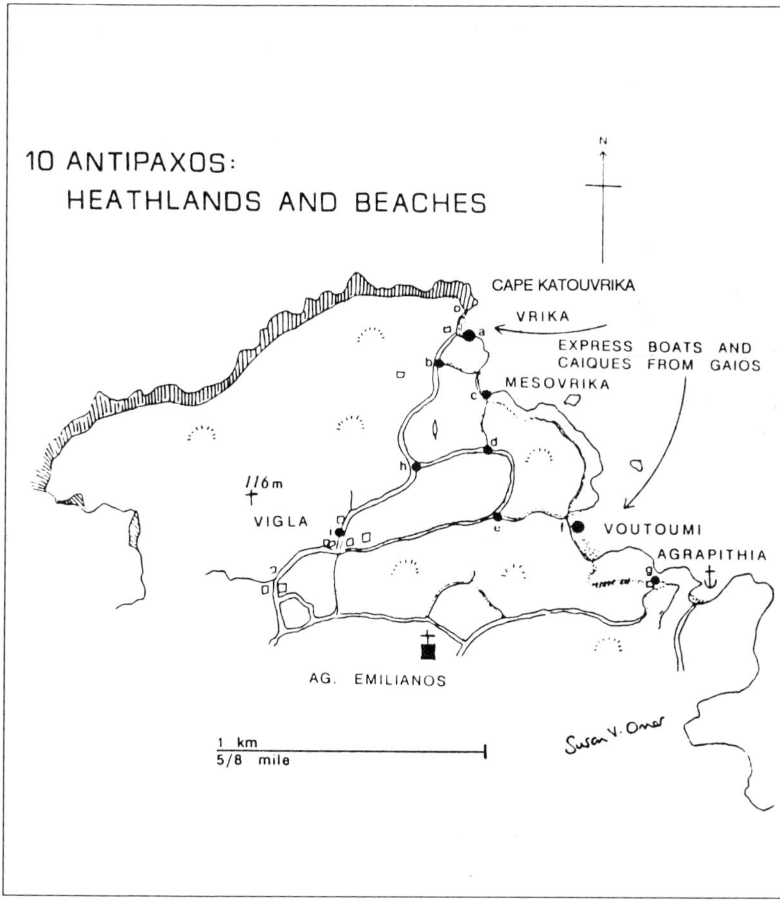

STARTING POINT: Vrika beach **[a]**

Check when and from where the boats to Paxos will return.

There are two tavernas on this beautiful sandy beach. Facing inland, **the path begins on the far side of the left hand taverna**. The track travels uphill in heathland and you will immediately appreciate the tranquility of Antipaxos: all to be heard will be the bubbling songs of larks and warblers; the buzz of insects and the faint lapping of waves. **About 50 yards after the taverna a track joins from the left [b]. Follow this to the secluded beach of Mesovrika. At the far (southern) end is a path [c] leading through some bushes uphill to a wide track [d]. Turn left.** This lane skirts the hill, offering a panoramic view of Paxos cliffs and the mainland. As you round the hill Voutoumi bay comes into sight below you **[f]**. The sand here is so amazingly fine and white that it is almost like flour. The smallest of creatures leaves its trail across the floor of the bay, from tiny claws of a baby crab to the fins of a flatfish. From your vantage point you can watch schools of rainbow coloured fish darting in the shallows. The sea is so clear that they appear to be swimming through air. You may wonder why the sea is such an extrordinary shade of turquoise? - it is because the white sandy floor of the bay is reflecting the azure of the Ionian sky. If you watch an occasional seagull flying over the bay, see how the white underside of the bird suddenly reflects the turquoise water as it passes over the sea.

The path to Voutoumi joins your track from below on your left [e]. A viewpoint taverna is reached on the far side of the bay via a short uphill path **[g]**. Voutoumi Beach offers unrivalled snorkeling around the rocks and there is a sea cave on the south side of the bay in which you can swim. The Paxiots frequently hunt for octopus here using tridents rather like the one belonging to the Greek god Poseidon - Ruler of the Seas. Legend tells how Poseidon used his trident to strike off the southern tip of Corfu and thus created Paxos as an idyllic retreat for himself and his beloved Amphitriti. His trident is now the emblem of Paxos and all the Ionian islands.

At the back of the beach is an area of brackish water, and here interesting birds and insects can be seen. Although St Paul's disciples Krispos and Gaios reputedly rid Paxos and Antipaxos of snakes, they have obviously returned as there is a thriving population on both islands. In Paxos the hedgehog (Greek SKANTZOHEEROS), introduced in 1903, and domestic cats (introduced by a merchant sea captain from Hios), dispatch a number of snakes.
After your swim there may be a boat to Gaios from Voutoumi, but you will probably like to walk to Vrika. Instead of taking the low path via Misovrika **an interesting return route is to continue on the high road until a fork [h].** If you have time, **take the left lane uphill to explore the charming village [i] of Vigla** and St Emilianos church at the top of the hill. As you can sea, **the track down to the right skirts a valley and returns you (via [b] to [a]) Vrika Bay**. You have a superb view from here of Vrika Bay and the cliffs (Greek GREMMOS), of (right to left) Kaltsionissi Island, Moggonisi Island and the white southern cliffs of Paxos which look rather like the 'Seven Sisters' chalk cliffs near Brighton on the south coast of England. On the journey back to Paxos, note the sharply folded strata of the limestone cliffs near to Vrika, and at Kaltsionissi you can observe the direction of prevailing winds by the 'windswept' appearance of the vegetation on the exposed limestone. The wind dessicates and kills buds and growing points of shrubs and trees on the windward side enabling only the leeward parts of the plants to grow. Thus you will see Juniper, for instance, growing in a creeping manner close to the rock face.

<u>TO RETURN</u>: By boat from
Vrika Beach or Voutoumi beach.

11. MILLER'S PATH TO KOUTSI WINDMILL 3/4 mile (1.2 km)

If you are walking down to Loggos from Fontana (walk 13) or you are on the way back from the tranquil beach at Kipos (walk 5), don't miss the chance to see the 'elusive windmill' which so many people see from odd bends in the tortuous road, but few manage to locate, as it seems to disappear into the olives upon approach! Windmills, now all semi-ruined on Paxos, were once centres of great activity. There were more than 16 windmills on the island for milling grain. Situated in the most exposed sites (to catch the sea breezes) windmills thereby command some of the best views on the island, making them doubly worthy of a visit. See also walks 17 and 19 which include windmills.

From the same starting point as walks 3, 4 and 5 starting 30 yards up the lane.

STARTING POINT: **[A]** By bus you will alight after Fontana en route to Loggos from Gaios. Ask for "*Kontogyinatika, sas parakalo*". **As you approach Loggos from Fontana by foot, look out for a white church** on the right on an S-bend leading downhill. **At the end of the right-hand bend the Kontogianatika olive press** (with the usual mound of fragrant pressed-olives residue outside) **is on the right. The walk begins opposite**, at the bus shelter and cluster of houses.

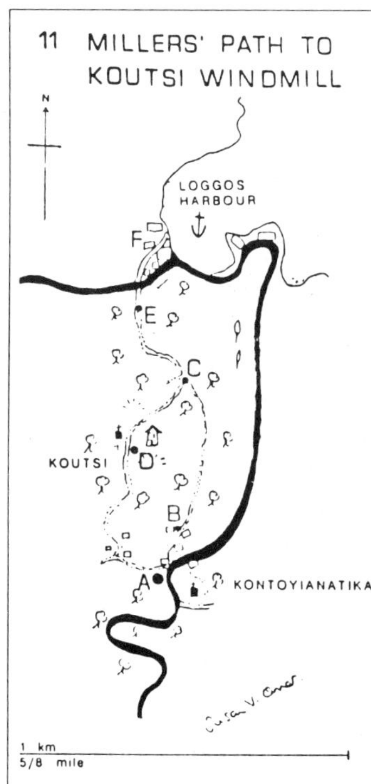

The ancient path of the Koutsi Millers leads up a small rise and down to Loggos. You will notice two tracks: the one on the left leads via Anemogianatika (bearing right and uphill) to the mill and church. **A second smaller path winds uphill past a couple of houses to the right of the main track [B]. Follow this path to the top of the rise** where it emerges into heathland **[C]. At the cross-paths turn sharp left to see the mill (70 yards). [D].** The path ahead peters out, **and the track to the right leads downhill to Loggos. This path bears right at a gate [E]** and brings you into the pretty harbour of Loggos **[F]**.

TO RETURN: By same route or take the bus from Loggos.

12 OLIVE PRESS TRACK TO ZENEBISSATIKA

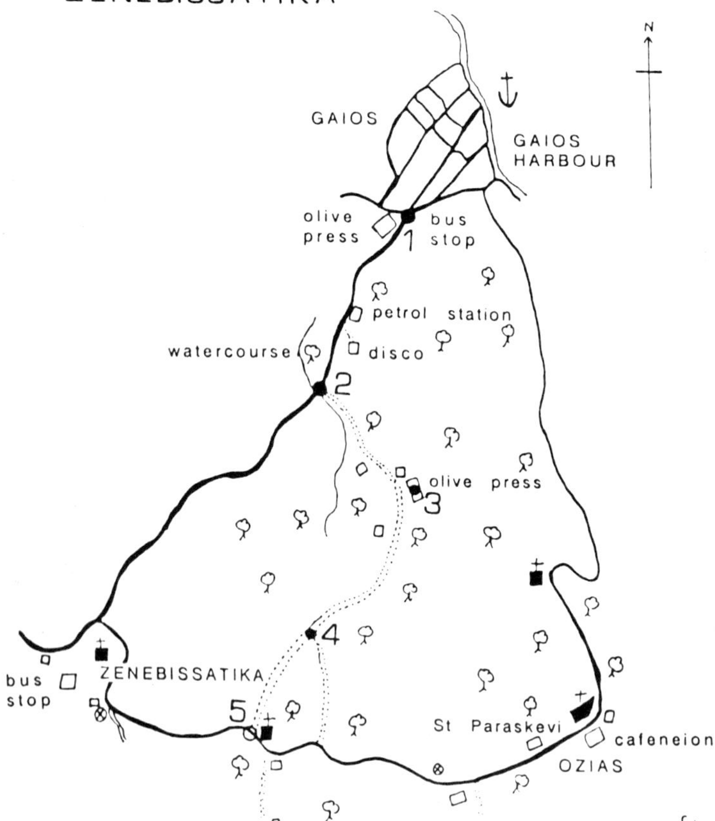

12. OLIVE PRESS TRACK TO ZENEBISSATIKA 7/8 mile (1.4 km)

To save you from walking up the hill following the road out of Gaios there is a charming walk through an olive grove which brings you to the starting point of a number of walks and is a useful short cut.

STARTING POINT: **Gaios bus stop [1]**

The road leaving Gaios forks. **Take the left lane with an olive press on your right.** After 100 yards you pass on your left the island's petrol station and then the Castello Disco. As the road bends uphill **you will see a dry watercourse passing under the road [2]. The well-defined stony track leads down to the left on the nearside of this bridge.** Following the track through the olives you pass an olive press on your left [3] and after another 100 yards bear **right [4] at a fork to reach the Zenebissatika-to-Ozias lane [5].** There is a small church on your left at the road junction.

FOR OZIAS 1/2 mile (0.8 km) turn left. Walks 19B and 1 begin there.

FOR VELLIANTATIKA and the bus stop turn right (3/8 mile or 0.6 km) for the start of walks 8, 16 and 22.

Olive Press

13. DONKEY PATH TO FONTANA

Walks Inland.

13. DONKEY PATH TO FONTANA 3/4 mile (1.2 km)

Fontana is a picturesque inland hamlet with several traditional coffee houses (cafeneions) situated around a square. A large stone village sterna with handpump (constructed during the English Protectorate) provides clean fresh water for which the local people make long treks.

From Fontana you can catch a bus to other parts of the island or walk down to the beaches of Loggos (walks 3, 4, 5, and 11).

STARTING POINT: **[A] St Charalambos Church, north of Bogdanatika** on the bus route from Gaios to Magazia. On the bus ask for "*Ayios Haralambos, sas parakalo*". Charalambos was the saint (Greek. AGHIOS, shortened to Ag.) who rid the island of a dreadful plague. The church dedicated to him has an enormously high baroque bell tower which was damaged by lightening in 1988 and is a favourite nesting site for swallows and martins.

From St Charlambos bell tower you have, on clear days, beautiful views southwards to Antipaxos, while Lefkada and Cephalonia appear to hover on the horizon over a hazy sea. After a storm these islands can be seen quite distinctly, but during the summer months even the mainland sometimes disappears behind a shroud of heat-haze.

With the church on your right, join a little lane just beyond the church on the right [B]. It goes steeply uphill and at the top of the rise **bends sharply to the left [C].** If you were to continue to the left you would reach the highest point on the island (813 feet or 248 metres) at St Issavros. The legendary Greek god Poseidon, Ruler of the Seas, left his great trident there at Megali Vigla (lit: Great lookout). In the days of Poseidon, Megali Vigla would indeed have been a superb vantage point. However, the Venetians have since planted the area with olive trees which now obscure the view. **At the bend in the lane is a walled path ahead. Follow this** through a landscape of terraced olives and after a minute you can see the Ionian Sea and the mainland to the east. In winter and early spring the snowcapped mainland mountains of Ipiros are exceptionally lovely.

The donkey trail takes you through most attractive peaceful countryside, gradually leading to the northeast (bearing left). On clear days you have a magnificent view northwards to Corfu (Kerkira) and Albania. You can pick out the white cliffs at Kavos in the south of Corfu and (from left to right) you will see the mountain tops of Ag. Georgias (392m); Ag. Mattheos (463m); Ag. Deka (576m), and in the distance Pantokrator ('the Almighty') which is the highest point in Corfu at 906 metres. The sunshine may highlight the eight mile sandy beach of Aghios Georgias to the west of the Kavos cliffs. To the east

you can see the lofty Albanian mountains in the distance, and jutting out in the middle distance is the headland at Sivota (Mourtos).
The track now becomes less well defined on a rocky ledge and you continue parallel to the olive terraces which follow the contours of the hill. The thickly wooded valley below you to the right is frequented by many warblers, shrikes and chats. On your left you pass an olive tree whose lower boughs have been propped up with three large rocks. From here **[D] the path descends over some natural rock steps** between small semi-circular retaining walls. You join a level concrete track at the bottom **[E] and turn left**. If you intend to return along this route take note of where your path joins the track (viz. just before the concrete section gives way to stones).

You are in a captivating landscape of hollowed and contorted olive trees growing in ordered rows in well-maintained terraces. These stone walls were built by skilled craftsmen during the Venetian Rule of 1386 to 1797. Each wall is an intricate three-dimensional jigsaw puzzle with the minimum of gaps between the stone blocks (yet there are sufficient shady niches for lizards, snakes and small mammals to hide in). You will probably see donkeys and goats tethered in the shade, and, if it is in the harvesting season, local women will be collecting olives from nets under the trees. This arduous task begins in November and continues through to June every second year on Paxos (and every winter on Corfu). The olives are allowed to fall of their own accord onto the nets where they are shaken into piles and the leaves and twigs picked out. Sacks containing more than 100 pounds (50 kilograms) of olives are conveyed by donkey along the trail to the local olive presses which are just outside Fontana.

The lane is joined by two lanes from the right (which lead to the coast at Kloni-Gouli, see walk 2). **To the left is Fontana square** with its pretty white campanile outside the church. [F].

TO RETURN: You can relax over a coffee or perhaps lemonade (Greek LEMONATHA, or PORTOKOLATHA for orangeade) outside the CAFENEION. Then you may **catch a bus or embark on the downhill walk to Loggos.**

14. SHADY LANE TO REMOTE IPAPANTI 2 1/4 miles (3.6 km)

On a hot day what could be more pleasant than a walk among shady olive groves carpeted with flowers to a little hamlet far above Lakka! At Ipapanti (also called Grammetika) you can climb a high bell tower with views to Lakka Bay and Corfu. The walk, which is uphill along broad tracks, continues to Magazia from where you can catch a bus.

From the same starting point as walks 6, 7, 17 and 18.

STARTING POINT: Lakka quayside [A]

Lakka harbour is bustling with exotic visitors in mid-August: flotillas of gleaming yachts anchor in the sundrenched harbour and the picturesque waterfront tavernas are thronging with life. At night Lakka is quaintly appealing, as visitors and locals alike relax and enjoy traditional Greek fare well into the small hours, seated in the little squares (Greek PLATEEA).

From the quayside **make your way to the bus stop.** From here two roads lead out of Lakka on either side of the white church. **Take the right hand lane.** You pass on your left a modern olive press and a side lane to the right (which leads to the lighthouse, walk 18) [B]. The lane ahead plunges into peaceful olive groves with a chance of seeing falcons, ravens and even the odd migrating eagle circling overhead. You pass a group of cottages and Aloni Disco before reaching **a fork in the road at an area of disturbed ground [C].** A dry watercourse is to your right. **Take the right hand lane** which follows the watercourse. After a storm the watercourses of Paxos suddenly become raging torrents which just as quickly vanish once more. Several days after a downpour flowers and lush grass seem to spring from the ground to mark the passing of the storm. You pass two side-tracks leading up to the right and continue upwards in hauntingly beautiful countryside where the odd ruined olive press can be spied between the twisted branches of the ancient silver-leafed olives.

You reach a level stretch and **a junction by a yellow-based house** on the left **[D]**. The lane to the right goes to Ipapanti and rejoins the main lane (ahead) further up. **Turn right up the concrete track** and turn right at a high wall ahead of you. Suddenly you are on a broad grassy ride looking directly at the magnificent 1772 Ipapanti bell tower.

This garden-like hillside village is entirely walled and paved with local honey-coloured limestone: flagstoned paths and broad flights of steps radiate from the centre. In the gardens are enormous fig trees and verdant-leafed lime and lemon trees. Purple Bougainvillea cascades over whitewashed cottages and even an introduced tropical palm

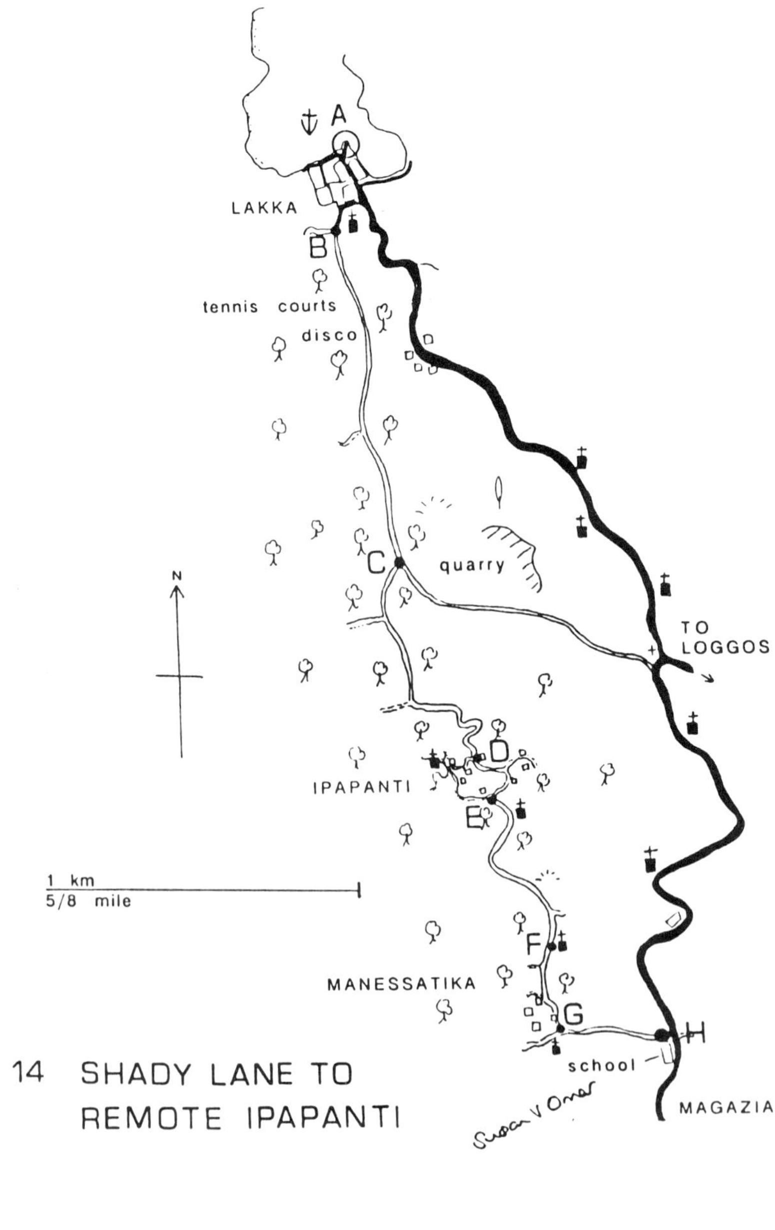

14 SHADY LANE TO REMOTE IPAPANTI

waves its spiky foliage. The backdrop is a valley of olives like an undulating silver-green sea leading to the blue bay of Lakka.

The church of Ipapanti (built in 1601) with its eye-catching orange walls is set in a flagstoned courtyard. Its two (unique) domes look rather like the funnels of a ship. The lower door to the separate baroque bell-tower is normally open and you can climb to the domed belfry which houses several nesting pairs of house martins most years. The view from the belfry over Lakka and to Corfu is marvellous.

In the foreground, the ground drops rapidly beyond the hamlet to a gulley which has a fresh-water spring. Beyond is a hillside clad with lichen-covered olives and towering cypresses.

To continue your walk: **uphill from the bell-tower is a broad flight of stone steps**, walled on either side. **After a few yards take a left hand walled path** which becomes narrow, leading around two gardens and **emerging at the main lane after some steps upwards [E].**

Turn to the right and follow the lane as it twists uphill, passing a side-lane to the left and a little chapel set back from the lane on the left **[F]**. You pass an area of sunny heath and cypresses and **reach a junction**. A lane leads down to the right amid very fine olive terraces. **Take the left lane uphill** and you soon reach a hamlet. Continuing along the hilltop you now , almost unexpectedly, reach the little village of Manessatika **[G]**. The lane which joins from the right leads to the Kastanitha clifftops and back to Lakka (walk 17 - 3 miles).

Keep straight ahead for the main lane at Magazia which is 1/4 mile (0.4 km) from here. You reach the main lane to the left of a school and opposite a baker **[H]**.

TO RETURN: You can catch the bus south to Gaios or north to Lakka (2 1/2 miles or 4 km).

The Church at Ipapanti

15. OSTRIAS WELLS AND VIEWPOINT. 3/8 mile (0.6 km)

A very short walk to ancient stone water pits and a well at an unexpected viewpoint overlooking the Bay of Prasses.

STARTING POINT: The doctors' clinic at Bogdanatika [1]. On the bus ask for *"Bogdanatika, sas parakalo"*. **The path starts opposite Bogdanatika chapel**, ie. the first church beyond the road junction going north.

Follow a walled path opposite the chapel. Bear right at a junction by a large olive tree [2] and follow a faint path through an olive grove with a steep-sided valley to your right **[3]**. In the spring and autumn the woodland floor is carpeted with wild flowers including pink cyclamens and waxy yellow crocuses.

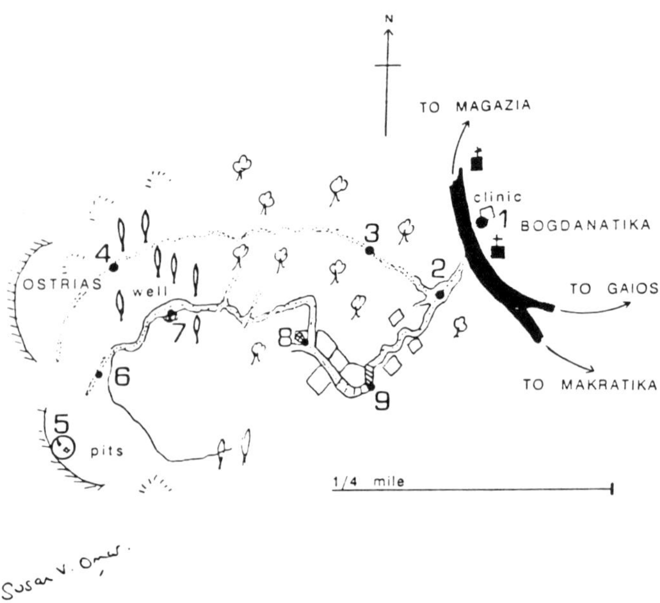

15 OSTRIAS WELLS AND VIEWPOINT

Walking west for only a few minutes **you reach a limestone pavement** where columnar cypresses grow in deep crevasses **[4]**. You can see old olive terraces on the opposite hillside, now reverting to heathland. The limestone plateau is a huge expanse of gleaming white rock - a breathtaking natural rockery and habitat for an abundance of delicate flowers and colourful butterflies. As you follow the platform, bearing left, Avlaki Creek (reached in walk 8) comes into view to the southwest and you discover the stone pits which are always water-filled **[5]**. These were once used as a water supply by the residents. This escarpment view is particularly stunning when acres of purple heather bloom in the autumn.

<u>TO RETURN</u>: **You will notice a wall at the top of the escarpment: with this on your right you will soon join a path** which broadens into a track and runs parallel to but higher than your outward route **[6]**.

You reach a stone water trough and a shelter built into the wall: it houses a deep well **[7]**. The well's cool interior is a daytime refuge for geckos (a type of lizard). You may see these pale animals emerging at night on taverna walls: they capture moths and other night-flying insects which are attracted to the lights. Greeks come to recognise individual geckos (even giving them pet names) and their presence in a home is said to bring luck to the household. They certainly capture numerous troublesome insects and offer 'in-house entertainment' while stalking insects on the wall in a patient cat-like manner, even lashing their little tails in a truly feline way before the final pounce! As well as their remarkably carrying "peeep-peep" voices, geckos are extraordinary for their feet which are like living 'crampons'. The undersides of the toes have fanwise flaps of skin covered in microscopic hooks that catch every slightest irregularity, even those in the surface of glass. Thus geckos can walk up walls and across ceilings, seeming to defy gravity. They can even walk across water.

The narrow walled path leads now into an olive grove. Keep ahead between the walls and, after passing a garden on the left, **turn right [8]**. The track leads between pretty stone houses and down a shallow flight of steps **[9]**. **You emerge at the solitary olive tree [2] from which you set out and the road is ahead**. If you turn left at the road you will have an interesting view through some railings of a restored olive mill: the two large stones are edge-running grinding wheels (Greek LITHARO) which rotate to crush olives.

<u>TO RETURN TO GAIOS</u>: You catch the bus or walk down the lane (1 mile or 1.6 km).

Gecco

16 TO MOUSMOULI CLIFFTOP

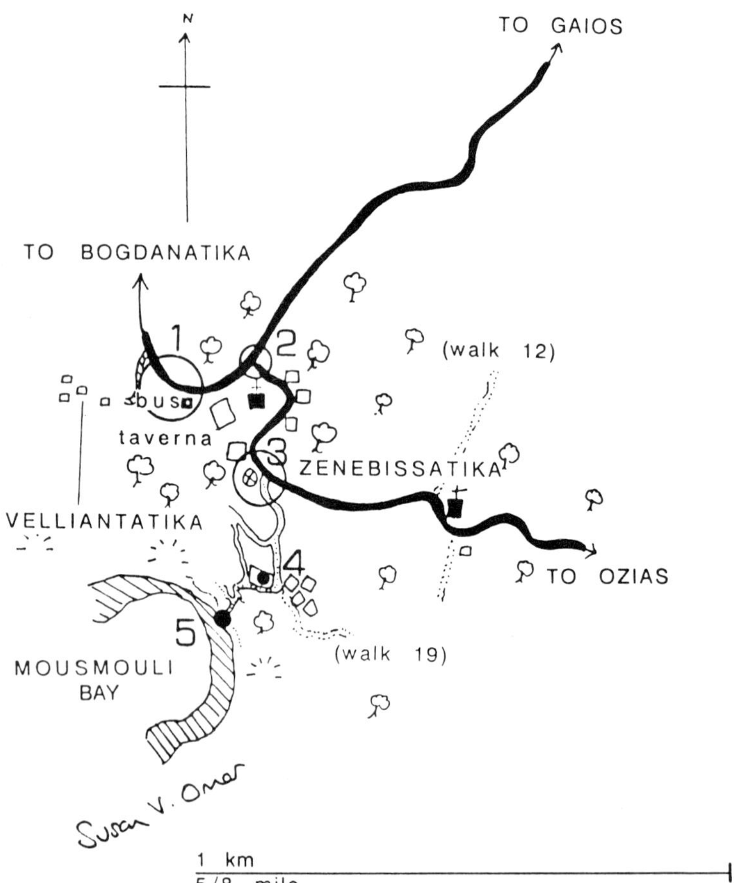

Walks to the Cliffs.

16. TO MOUSMOULI 3/8 mile (0.6 km)

On Greek maps look for GREMMOS (= cliffs) and AKROTIRION, shortened to Akr. (= cape or headland).

This is a very short and easy walk with a superb view from a clifftop from where you may like to watch the fiery Ionian sun set over a calm sea. It is a lovely spot for a picnic.

From the same starting point as walks 8 and 22.

STARTING POINT: [1] The bus stop and taverna at Zenebissatika which is **on the point of a 90° right hand bend one mile outside of Gaios** on the Makratika road.

From the taverna **take the Ozias road (facing downhill, this leads off the main road to the right) [2].** You pass several houses and on the right reach a fine village sterna with hand pump **[3]. The road forks here: take the right hand lane uphill** and follow it to the end by one of the island's many olive presses (Greek LITROUVIO) which is on the right **[4]**. The pile of residue from crushed olives seen outside every working press has many uses. It is normally conveyed to the mainland from Paxos and used as a fertiliser for crops and sometimes it is used as a material in road construction. Often the fragrant residue is shovelled into an open boiler in olive presses and burned to heat the water which is part of the oil separation system: an example of a very neat self-contained energy cycle evolved through necessity (as there is little else to burn on the island).

Behind the olive press follow a walled path (joined after 15 yards by a second walled path from Velliantatika on the right) and continue straight ahead. The track is often overhung with olive nets set at an angle to allow the ripe olives to roll down into a collecting net on the right. **You suddenly emerge from the trees at a cliff top** overlooking the inaccessible bay of Mousmouli **[5].**

<u>TO RETURN</u>: You can walk to the **Windmill and Tripitos Arch** from the olive press (walk 19); perhaps you will want to walk back to Gaios via the **Olive Press track** (walk 12) **or wait for a bus.**

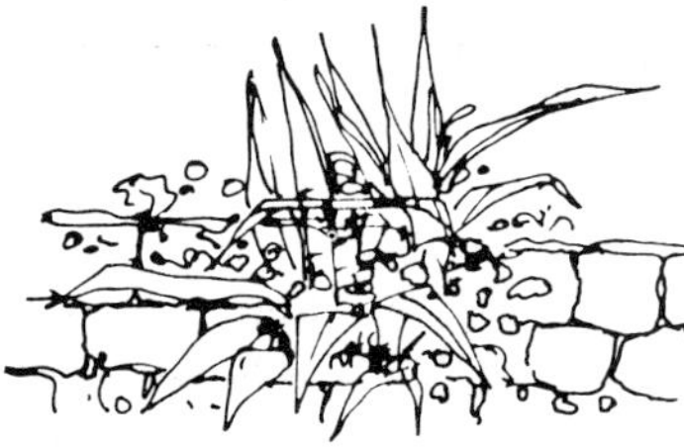

Walks to the Cliffs.

17. VASSILATIKA "FORGOTTEN VILLAGE" AND WINDMILL 3 miles (4.8 km)

Hidden at the top of a wooded hillside is the 'forgotten village' of Vassilatika with a number of fine Venetian houses The path leads to Kastanitha cliffs and a lovely old windmill. This particularly spectacular walk ends in Magazia with an option to return to Lakka via walk 14 or catch a bus.

From the same starting point as walks 6 and 7.

STARTING POINT: **Lakka quayside [A]**

Walk to the bus stop in Lakka and take the right hand lane leading to the south with a white church on your left **[B]**. The priest's patient little donkey may be dozing in the shade outside the churchyard. You pass an olive factory on the left and a side lane to the right (which leads to Lakka lighthouse, see walk 18). **Continue ahead** through the olive groves until you reach **a side track leading over a dry watercourse and steeply uphill to the right [C]**. Take this concrete track up a rise to open heathland where the track turns back downhill to the right. **Depart from the track here and continue up ahead** along a rough sunny track where you will come across a fascinating ruined olive press (Greek LITROUVIO) on your right **[D]**. Inside are still the huge stone grinding wheels (Greek LITHARO) and wooden spindles (Greek ATHRAKTIA) which formed part of the primitive press. The olive oil is then poured into a catchment pit (Greek KATOLAVRI). You will see many old-style presses on the island in addition to the modern ones which nowadays use much the same labour-intensive methods. From the island's estimated 25,000 privately owned olive trees the output of oil reaches 4,000 tons every second year.

Just after the press, on the top of the heathland rise, a crosspaths with a large concrete tank is ahead on the right. **Cross straight over the broad track to join a narrow walled path** which meanders through an olive grove with a field to your left. Walking to the right of a watercourse you soon **climb some steps leading up to the right** and the track then takes you past a group of stone buildings and a cottage with pink gates. Here on a garden wall is a row of Paxos ribbed urns (traditionally used for storing water) which have been amusingly painted with rainbow stripes. **Join the lane ahead** which leads to Lakka to the right (1 mile or 1.6 km) and Vassilatika to the left (3/8 mile or 0.6 km) **[E]**.

Turn to the left. You pass a shrine and continue along the hilltop. A track joins from the right and here you can see some of the famous

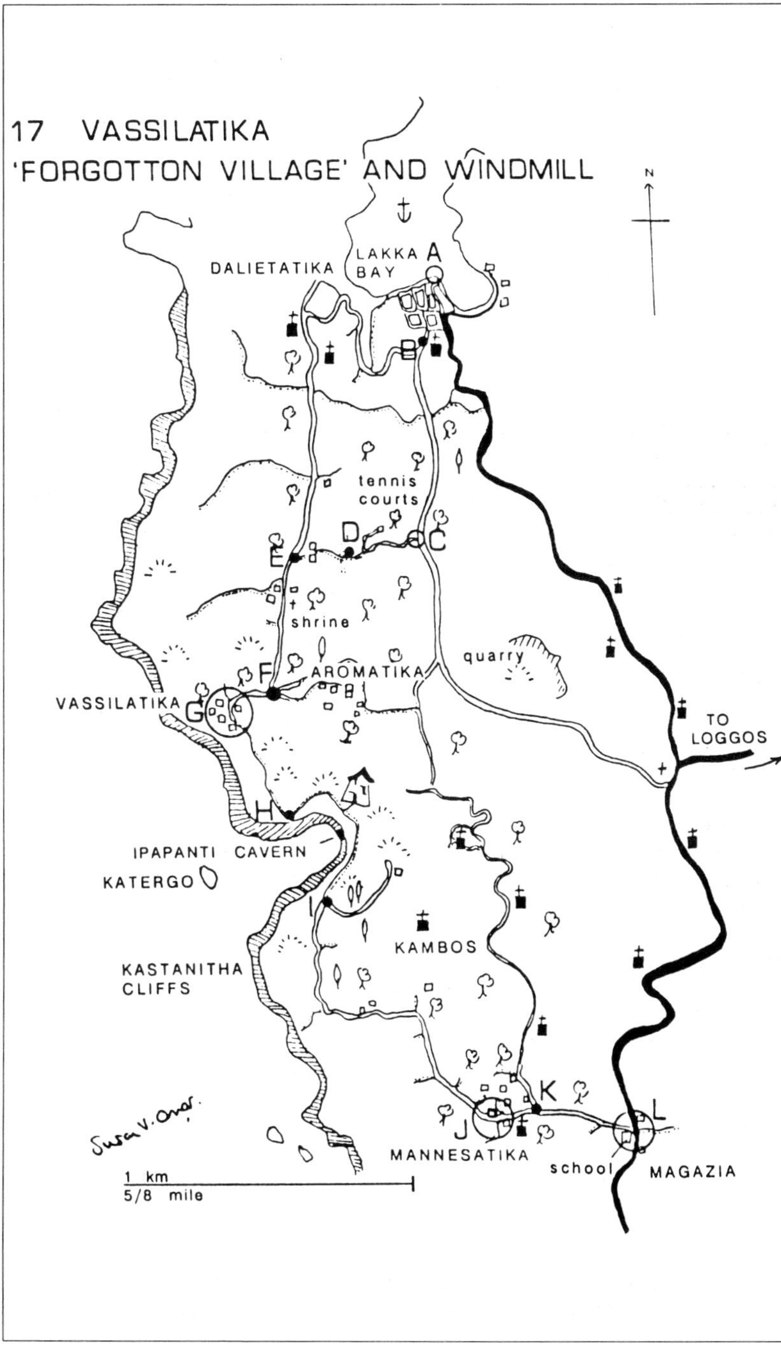

17 VASSILATIKA
'FORGOTTON VILLAGE' AND WINDMILL
N
LAKKA BAY
A
DALIETATIKA
B
tennis courts
D
C
E
shrine
quarry
F
AROMATIKA
VASSILATIKA
G
TO LOGGOS
H
IPAPANTI CAVERN
KATERGO
I
KAMBOS
KASTANITHA CLIFFS
K
J
L
MANNESATIKA
school
MAGAZIA
1 km
5/8 mile

prickly pear cactus bushes whose aptly-named reddish fruits are eaten in October. As you progress along the concrete track ahead, two lanes join from below you on the left. The track enters some delightful heathland (Greek REEKIA) with views to the limestone quarry above Lakka. Freshly exposed limestone is a gleaming white, but inland the surfaces soon weather to a more mellow golden. Wending its way uphill the little **lane reaches the village** (Greek HORRIO) **of Vassilatika [G].**

Although known as a deserted or forsaken village, there are now several families living here. There is an old olive press on the right, outside which donkeys (conveying several heavy sacks of olives) used to relax when relieved of their burdens. You can see the stone-carved tethering rings set in the wall. The donkeys would have a drink of water before trekking back into the olive groves with the hardworking olive gatherers, who then, as now, were usually women and children on Paxos.

An ornate blue and white archway ahead of you is the entrance to a Venetian manor house. **The lane ends here**, but you **continue along a walled and shady track.** Presently **you emerge from the trees onto a beautiful heathland cliff top [H].** The path leads through somewhat prickly scrub right to the cliff edge from where you have a spectacular view of KASTINITHA cliffs below and ahead of you. Indigo waters lap at the base of the sheer white cliffs far (very far) below you. **Do not go too near the edge!** The famous IPAPANTI CAVERN (Greek SPILLIA = cavern, shortened to Sp. eg. Sp. Ipapanti) can be seen to the left. As the Paxiots will tell you, 'Papanickolos' a Greek submarine hid here between successful night sorties during the Second World War. You can visit this cavern by boat.

The path veers left around the cliff edge and at the top of a heathery rise you will see **the windmill on the left** which is worth a visit with its views over the island to the east coast. **Then rejoin the stoney cliff path which descends, joining a wall on the left. It leads to a wide track [I]. Turn right.** You now have a view across the bay to the clifftops you have just skirted - not a spot at which to linger for those suffering from vertigo! Reached by a now deteriorated path are some cunningly designed stone dwellings hidden in the cliffs near here. To these the Paxiots resorted during the days of piracy in the Middle Ages. They would lie in wait for the Corsair pirates. The Paxiots would open fire on them as they scrambled up the Kastanitha cliffs, with the intention to pillage the island and sieze young women for wives and men as slaves. The ever-resourceful Paxiots used to toss the unwelcome intruders over the cliffs.

The concrete track leads amongst olive groves and cypress trees **southwards**, with odd glimpses to the left of the opposite east coast of Paxos, and on the right, the nearby west coast. **Ignore any side lanes**

and soon the walled concrete path narrows. A white house with a blue door is on the left and a narrow track to the right **[J]**. **Turn left and you emerge on the Manesatika lane**, passing a church on the right. A little further on, in the centre of Manesatika, a lane joins from the left **[K]**.

OPTION: **Turn left for a downhill shady walk via Ipapanti to Lakka (walk 14 - 2 1/4 miles or 3.6 km).**

Take the right hand lane after 1/4 mile (0.4 km) to join the main bus route at Magazia [L].

RETURN: Lakka (left) is 2 1/2 miles (4 km) downhill. *NOTE: The bus only passes this point on journeys direct from Gaios to Lakka (or vice versa).* When the route includes Loggos the nearest bus stop is nearly 1 mile (1.6 km) towards Lakka (left) or turning right towards Gaios the bus stop is under 1/2 mile (0.8 km).

Lizzard

Hoopoe

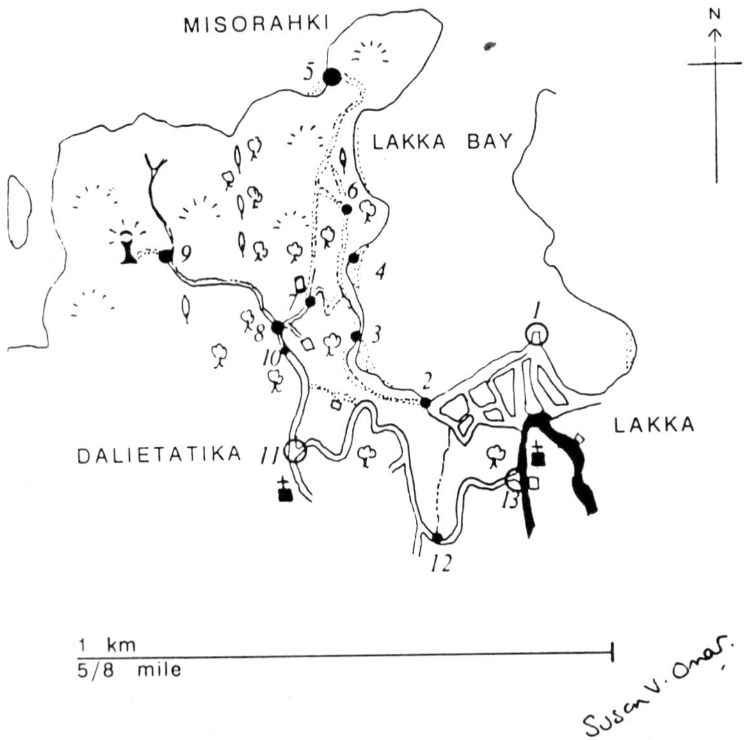

18 LAKKA LIGHTHOUSE AND HEADLAND

Walks to Cliffs.

18. LAKKA LIGHTHOUSE AND HEADLAND
1 3/4 miles (2.8 km), round trip

Lakka lighthouse is situated on the western arm of Lakka Headland. This easy walk from Lakka Beach includes very fine views from the cape to Lakka Bay, Corfu and Ipiros.

From the same starting point as walks 6, 7, 14 and 17.

STARTING POINT: The quayside in Lakka [1].

With the water on your right, make your way to the end of the harbour. **You will find a path starting by the sea** next to a waterfront taverna **[2]. It leads to the first bay [3]. Continue along the path** through the olive trees **to a second little bay [4]**. This is a perfect spot for swimming, sunbathing and windsurfing. The beach (Greek PARALEEA) is stony but the floor of the sea is sandy. **The path continues** up into scrub and heathland **at the far end of the beach. If you want to walk to the headland** (Greek AKROTIRI) from where there are commanding views, **continue north along the path ahead**. There is a little beach there on the exposed west side **[5].**

For the lighthouse you should turn left uphill at a fork in the path **[6]**, and over a collapsed fence to the **ridge-top path. Turn left here** and follow the trail on the level into an olive grove. You reach a house on your right (and a track zig-zags back down to the beach from here) **[7]**. You join the driveway of the house and this takes you after a few yards **to a crosspaths [8]. For a worthwhile view of the lighthouse, turn sharp right** (slightly uphill) for a pleasant hilltop walk over a heathland buzzing with insects. **Shortly you will reach the lighthouse** (Greek PHAROS) on your left **[9]**. It is surrounded by a high wall. **Now return to the crosspaths [8]** and this time **take the righthand arm southwards** (it leads slightly upwards) **[10]. You join another lane at the point of a hairpin bend.** To the right is the uphill route to Vassilatika (walk 17). **Take the left turning downhill [11].** You will pass four hairpin bends and two side-lanes join the track from the right.

TO RETURN: Just after the second side-lane you will notice a **stepped path leading downhill** on the left beside a wall **[12]** and **this is a short-cut into the centre of Lakka**. If you continue along the lane, then **turn left at the olive factory T-junction** at the foot of the hill **[13]** to arrive at Lakka bus stop.

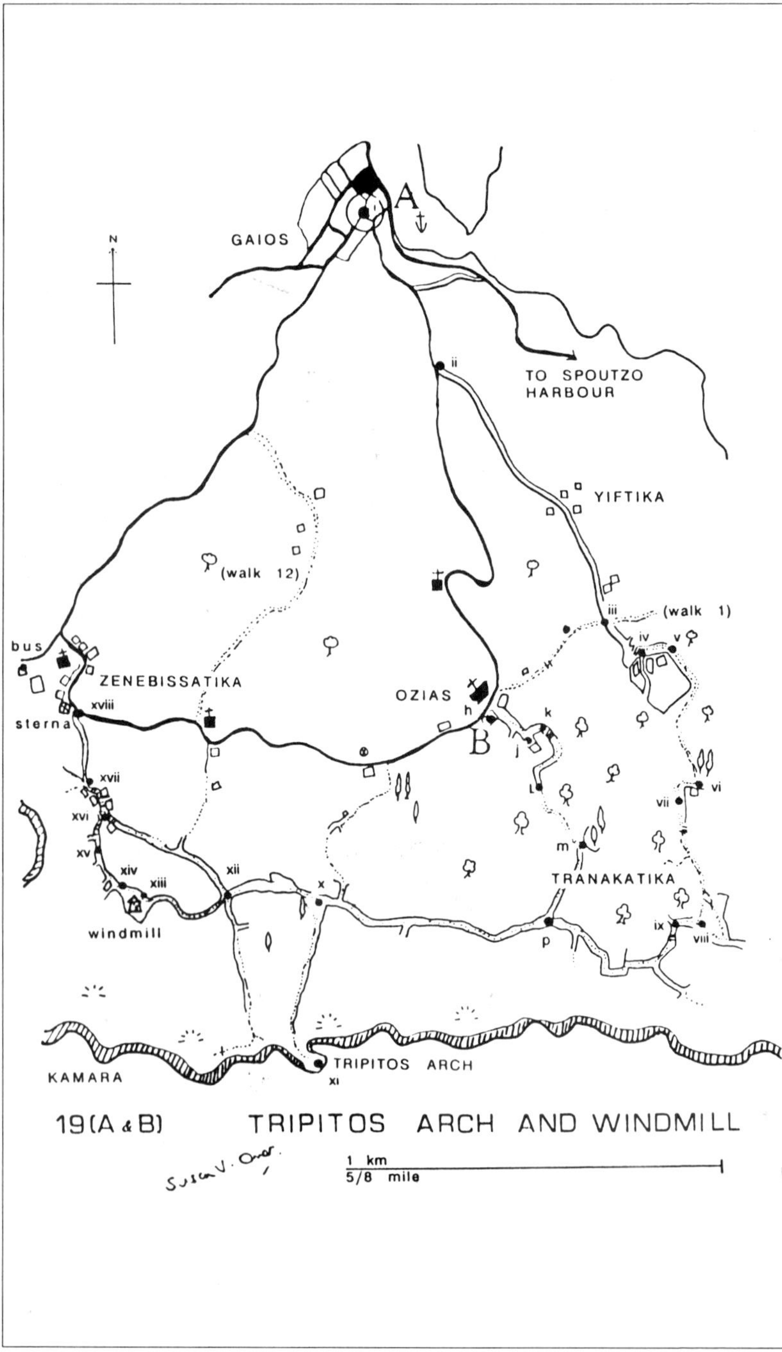

19(A & B) TRIPITOS ARCH AND WINDMILL

19A and 19B TRIPITOS ARCH AND WINDMILL

From Gaios (19 A) 3 1/4 miles (5.2 km)
From Ozias (19 B) 1 5/8 miles (2.6 km)

This pleasant ramble along the southwest coast of Paxos is along peaceful and secluded walled paths. The walk takes you to the fine limestone arch of TRIPITOS and you can actually walk all the way across the top. Visiting a windmill next, the walk ends in Velliantatika.

Limestone characteristically erodes with the passing of time along planes of weakness (faults) in the rock structure. It is due to this that Paxos has ten or more large sea caverns. When the sea carves a cavern (Greek SPILLIA) in a narrow headland, the pounding waves eventually wear back the cavern walls until a complete tunnel is formed under the headland. This tunnel enlarges continuously into a natural arch. The roof of the arch may eventually collapse leaving the seaward strut of the arch as a lonely rock pillar or stack. Such a stack on the west coast is ORTHOLITHOS (Greek ORTHOS= erect; LITHOS= stone), which can be seen from walk 20. TRIPITOS (Greek TRIPPA= cavity) is a fine example of a limestone arch on its 'last legs' before the roof caves in.

STARTING POINT:
19 A - GAIOS. Police Station Square, near the Post Office.
19 B - OZIAS. From the same starting point as Walk 1. Ozias Cafeneion opposite St Paraskevi Church..

WALK 19 A TO "P"
See also walk 1. From the Police Station the road to Ozias leads southwards inland [i]. After 200 yards you reach, in an olive grove, **a turn-off to the left** along a valley floor **[ii]**. Follow this concrete road to the 'gipsy village' of YIFTIKA (Greek YIFTOS= gipsy).

OPTION: **The path from Ozias to Moggonisi** (walk 1) crosses this lane **[iii]**.

Continue to the road terminus [iv]. Here, by some houses, you **take a white walled path up some steps to the left** with a house on the right. The walled pathway opens onto an olive grove **[v]. Turn right and uphill alongside the wall on your right.** Chickens are often scratching around in the dry olive leaves while tethered goats and donkeys lie in the shade. **The open path now continues upwards to a grove of cypress trees [vi]. A stone building with a green gate set in a wall is ahead of you. Turn right to follow a now distinct little path** (Greek THROMAKI) **uphill in the olives alongside the wall which is on your left (vii).** You go up a couple of stone steps and **continue directly**

ahead until **the path branches at a cypress grove** with an orange chicken run in the clearing ahead. **Turn right [viii]**. You meet a broad track. **Turn right** into the walled section which leads gently uphill. There is a view of the sea to the south.

At a T-junction [ix] in the walled path **turn left uphill** over some stone steps in an olive grove. A walled path joins from the sea cliffs on the left. Here you might hear the lonely "Ark-Ark" of a Paxos raven, probably nesting on a cliff ledge. As you continue up the path you have fine views to the left (southwards) of ANTIPAXOS. Growing along the wayside path you will find several Kermes oak trees, also known as holly oak (Quercus coccifera) with small, holly-like leaves and acorns. This is a common shrubby tree of the Mediterranean. Also look out for the once-important Carob tree (Ceratonia siliqua) with its compound leaves. The Carob (Greek KOUTSOUPEEA or HAROOPIA) is a member of the pea family and has flowers like those of the sweet pea. Its long thin pods contain small black seeds (Carobs or Locust Beans) which were the original jeweller's carat. The pods were until recently fed to livestock on Paxos and Antipaxos, and the beans are a favourite (strongly flavoured) sweet of the local people. Nowadays no-one harvests the Carob pods (the donkeys, sheep and goats being supplied with imported fodder), but elsewhere in the Mediterranean and in the Middle East, Carob is used for confectionary as a substitute for chocolate.

Over the heathland to your left are views over the sea and soon the pleasant walled path reaches a junction. **The walled path from Ozias (walk 19 B) joins from the right. Continue straight ahead for TRIPITOS [P].**

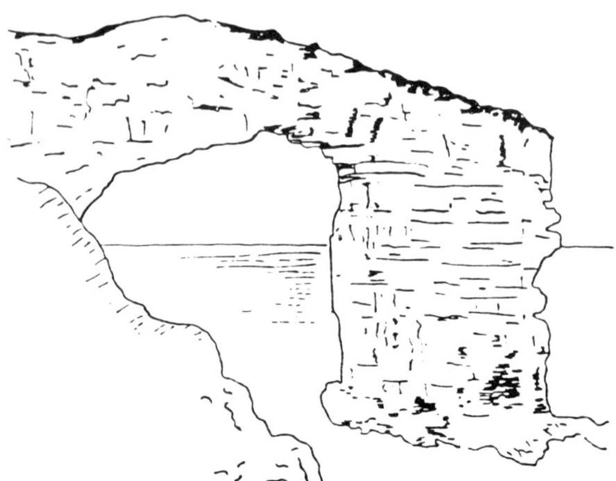

The Arch at Tripitos

<u>**WALKS 19 A and 19 B combine here at "P"**</u> - *(Start of walk 19 B is at the end of section* **[P]***)*

A path joins from the left and **then one from the right** (which also leads back towards Ozias). **After 10 yards you meet a walled** and somewhat overgrown **path on the left [x]**. The right hand wall has crumbled away. **This path leads directly to the cliff edge and Tripitos Arch [xi]**, across which you can walk **if you are careful**. It is dangerous to try to climb down to the sea because rocks are loose and crumbly, although local people, for reasons of their own, do so. Sitting precariously on the roof of the arch with the sea churning underneath you, you have a bird's eye view of huge schools of multi-coloured fish swimming in the translucent indigo waters.

Now return along the path to rejoin the principal track [x] where you **turn left**. After a minute or two **you reach an intersection** of walled paths with a blue gate set in the wall on your left **[xii]**. There are three tracks: the broad one on the right leads to Veliantatika, while a **centre path leads to the windmill** and then Veliantatika, and on the left is a blind-ending route to the cliffs.

Take the centre little track (Greek THROMAKI) **uphill**. It becomes narrow in an olive grove and bends to the right. Suddenly **you emerge in a beautiful sunny glade [xiii]**. The magnificent ruined mill (Greek MEELOS) towers in the centre of the glade with only a solitary tree for company. It has a fine arched doorway and a spiral stone staircase inside which you can climb for an unexpected view eastwards to the island of Panayia (Virgin Mary) near Gaios with its white lighthouse and monastery visible against a backdrop of azure sea and the mainland mountains of Ipiros. Antipaxos is also visible to the south from this lookout point.

Surrounded by olive groves, this grassy clearing is a haven for butterflies. **The path to Veliantatika begins at the north end of the glade** (viz. with the now unseen view of Panayia on your right). **The low-walled path among** olive terraces **divides into three with a concrete building to your left [xiv]. Keep to the path on the right here,** joining a distinct walled track leading downhill past a fig tree on the right.

The path bears right and leads down an intermittent flight of stone steps [xv]. Do not take any side turnings. Amongst some cottages you reach the bottom of the steps at a T-junction **[xvi]**. A white house with green shutters is in front of you. Turn left **down the steps between the houses and left again at a fork to reach the road below [xvii]**.

OPTION: As you emerge onto the lane, an olive press is ahead of you behind which the walk to Mousmouli cliffs (walk 16) begins.

The lane, which begins here, **leads directly to a village sterna** (water tank) **where it joins the road from Ozias** (right 3/4 mile or 1.2 km) to Zenebissatika **[xviii]**.

RETURN : Turn right for the Olive Press Walk to Gaios (walk 12, 1 1/8 miles or 1.8 km). Turn left for the taverna and bus stop at Zenebissatika from which walks 15 and 22 begin. For Gaios by road, turn left and at the T-junction by the taverna turn right (1 mile or 1.6 km downhill).

---

19 B OZIAS TO TRIPITOS ARCH AND WINDMILL
1 5/8 miles (2.6 km)

STARTING POINT: Ozias Cafeneion (see also walk 1).

For a shorter walk to the windmill and the arch at TRIPITOS, start out from **the Cafeneion opposite St Paraskevi Church in Ozias [h] On the left of the cafe is a walled path which leads to a red gate [j]. Turn left and then bear right at a junction along a walled path [k].** The path ends in an olive grove **[l]. Turn left uphill** and **walk 40 yards to a stand of mature cypress trees in a walled enclosure [m]**. With these trees on your left, **follow a narrow rocky walled path uphill.** After a minute you **bear right** at the start of a broad walled track on level ground. **You reach a T-junction 'P'** with a view of the windmill in the distance to the right. **Turn right** and **now follow the directions in Walk 19 A from 'P'.**

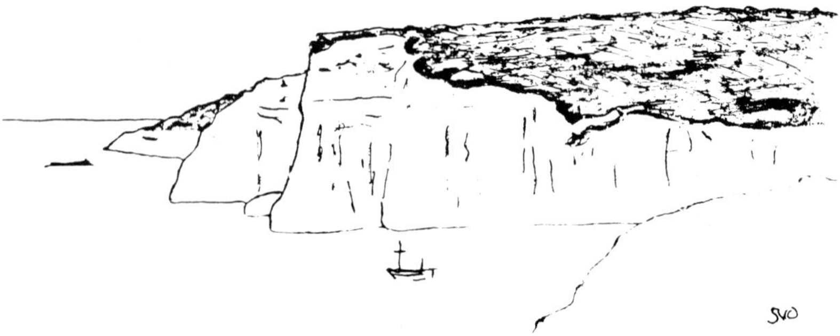

Ermitis Cliffs, as seen from walk 20

20 THE SAINTS OF THE APOSTLES AND SUNSET CLIFFS. 1 1/4 miles (2 km)

The quaint little church of the Saints of the Apostles commands a unique view of Ermitis cliffs which should not be missed. Further on are panoramic clifftop views of much of the west coast cliffs to the north and south. An easy track goes all the way.

<u>STARTING POINT</u>: **Magazia, the bus stop [a].** Going from Gaios this is at the road junction for Loggos.

From Gaios the bus stops in Magazia at a righthand road junction to Loggos. **Magazia Church is on the right (facing north)** just before the turnoff. **Opposite the church is a lane leading downhill [b]. Follow this track to Boiikatika, a hamlet 3/4 mile (1.2 km) away [c].** The woodland scenery is delightful and offers glimpses of an azure sea to the left.

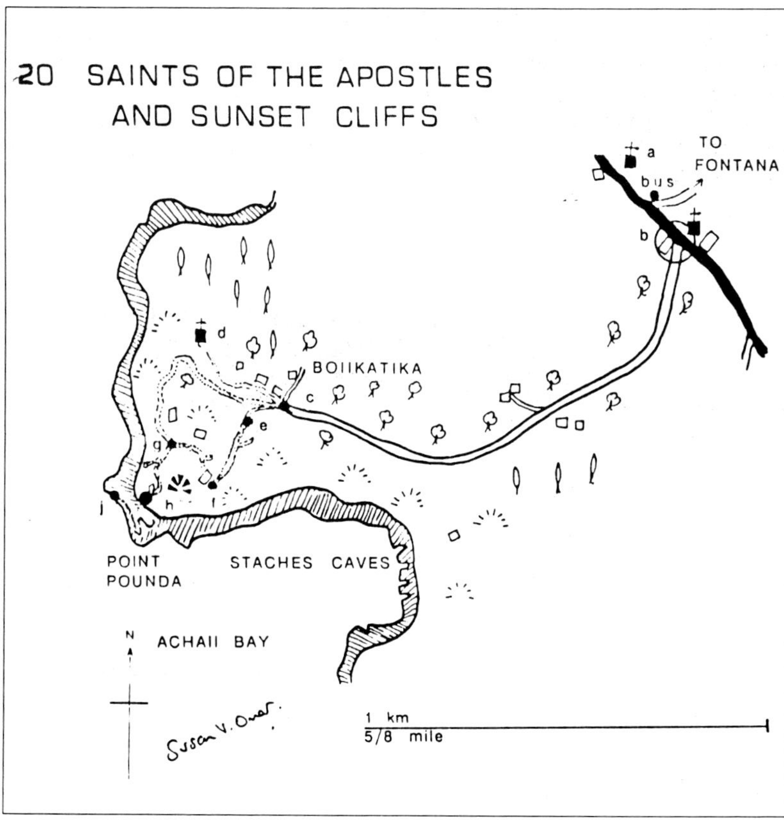

At the end of the track turn right for the church [d]. Saints Apostoli has no bell tower or campanile - the bell hangs with simple grace in an olive tree in the churchyard. This is a serene and beautiful setting for a spectacular view of Ermitis Cliffs from the corner of the churchyard. Please close the churchyard gate to keep out the local goats which are normally hobbled, not tethered, in this area.

Return to the track [c] and now **take the left of two downhill lanes [e].** You wander out of the olive groves into sunny heathland which throngs with migrating songbirds in spring and autumn. Shy grouse (Greek PERTHIKA) feed on young heather shoots, and on sunny days lizards, numerous butterflies and sometimes basking snakes will be seen.

Continue downhill to the end of the track by a new stone house with blue shutters (on the right) **[f]. To reach the headland** (Greek AKROTIRI or Akr.) you can follow a rather overgrown walled path ahead or, preferably, **join a concrete track beginning behind the house. It leads downhill and at a fork you should turn left [g].** You pass a side track to the right and then pass a concrete building. **The track ends [h] and a path leads ahead** through scrubland **down to a limestone platform at sea level** where succulent cushions of sea pink (campion) seem to flourish in their harsh environment in the rock crevasses **[j]**. This path is, however, very steep and swimming is not recommended from the rocks as they have been undercut by the sea. *(Having jumped in, maybe you will be unable to get out).*

From the top of the headland (Akr. Pounda) you have an inspiring view (Greek THAYA) of caves, cliffs, heathland, sandy inaccessible beaches, Antipaxos and mile upon mile of pure blue sea. If you look hard at the sea you may see odd patterns, like roads, streaking the surface. The Paxiots will tell you that when there are 'lanes in the sea' bad weather is on its way, and they are probably correct, for these stripes are shadows of thin whispy cirrus clouds more than 40,000 feet (1,200 metres) high and invisible to the eye against the glare of the sky. These clouds are the fore-runners of climatic depressions which are rare in the summer months.

The view: Corfu (KERKYRA) is visible to the north beyond the cliffs of Ermitis. To the south is Achaii Bay with five partly collapsed sea caverns (Greek SPILLIA or Sp.) known as Sp. Staches, and beyond is Achandakas Headland. Towering beyond Akr. Achandakas is a rare view from the land of Ortholithos stack which guards the entrance to Petriti cavern, into which even large boats can sail.

TO RETURN: The easiest route **back to Magazia** is **the way you came.** The shade provided by the olive groves will be welcomed on a hot day. You may like to drink coffee at a Cafeneion in Magazia while waiting for your bus, or visit one of the small grocery shops which sell fresh produce including golden-yolked free-range eggs and clear honey for which Paxos is renowned.

21. VLACHOPOULATIKA VIEWPOINT. 3/4 mile (1.2 km)

This is an interesting diversion from the principal walk from Vlachopoulatika which is to the little creek (walk 9).

From the same starting point as walks 2 and 9.

STARTING POINT: **Vlachopoulatika bus stop [A]. You take the lane past the football pitch [B] to Vlachopoulatika from the bus stop on the main road.** By turning neither right nor left you soon reach the charming village and **the lane bears to the left in the village** at a square **[C]. The lane finally ends in front of a white-washed house [D].**

OPTION: Turn right here for walk 9.

Turn left along a walled path past some juniper trees and **through a little gate** leading into an olive grove. After only a few yards **you reach a natural viewing platform [X]** from which you can see Antipaxos and the Bay of Prasses including Avlaki Creek (walk 8); Fanariotatika Headland (walk 22); and the cliffs of Mousmouli Bay (walk 16).

TO RETURN: You may decide to complete **walk 9 to the Pirates Creek or return to the starting point** for a refreshing drink at the taverna while waiting for the bus to Gaios (which is 1 1/4 miles or 2 km by road from the taverna).

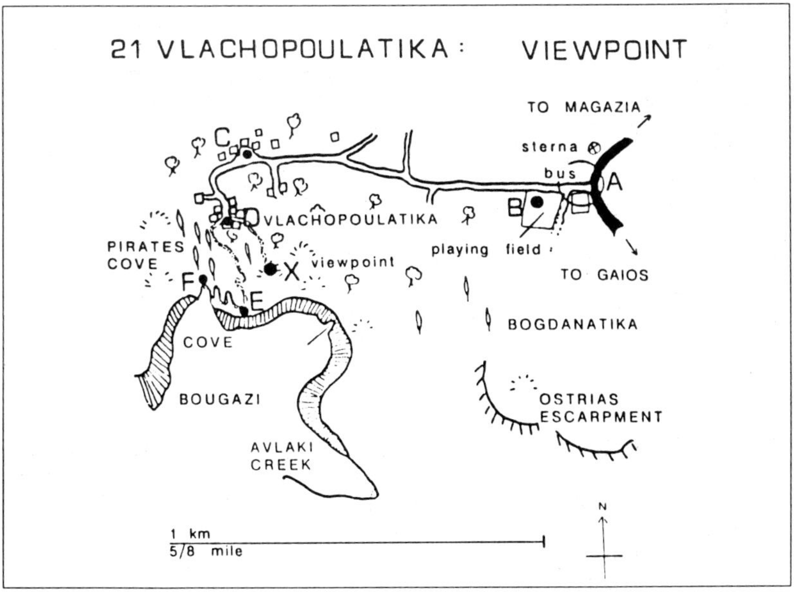

22 FANARIOTATIKA HEADLAND

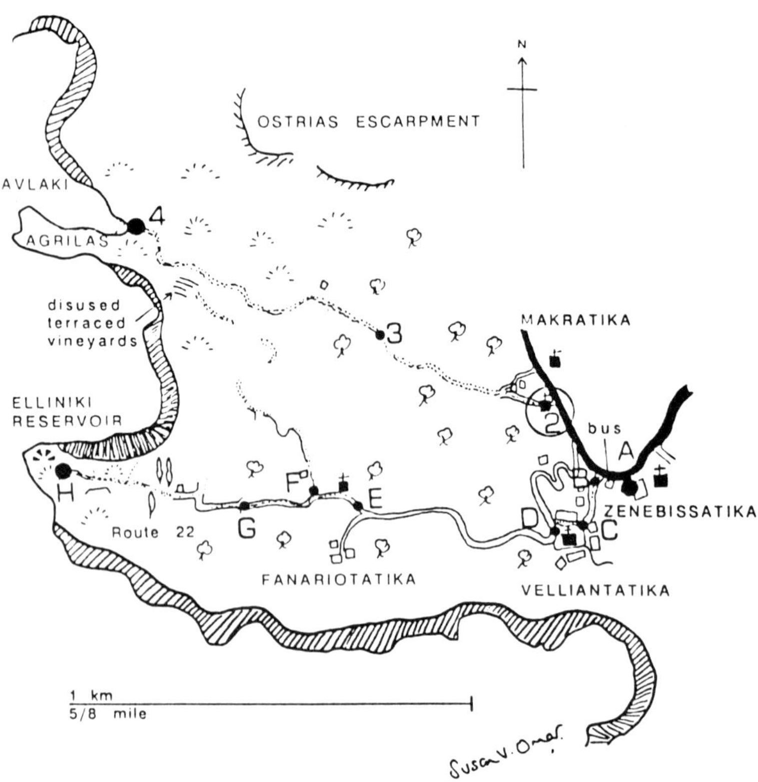

Walks to Cliffs.

22. FANARIOTATIKA HEADLAND 1 mile (1.6 km)

This easy level walk to a beautiful west coast headland should not be missed, especially if you are staying near Velliantatika.

From the same starting point as walks 8 and 16.

STARTING POINT: **The bus stop and taverna at Zenebissatika, 1 mile (1.6 km) from Gaios on the Makratika road [A].**

The bus stop is adjacent to a friendly taverna, on a bend in the road. **Next to the bus shelter**, looking uphill, **is a walled path on the left [B]. Follow this up some steps** past a couple of fine Venetian villas with flagstoned courtyards. **At the top of the rise bear left** and you come to a small square or courtyard between two sets of old-style terraced cottages with white-washed walls and gaily-coloured shutters [C]. During seista time in summer, villages like this one are totally silent as the Paxiots shelter from the searing sun (and there is actually a law against playing music, revving motorbike engines or otherwise disturbing the peace at these times). **Take a track on the right** with a walled garden (Greek KEEPA) on the left and an interesting olive press on the right. This has three stone grinding wheels (Greek LITHARO) which rotate around a central axis. If you are lucky enough to visit Paxos during an olive-harvesting season you should not miss an opportunity to see such a press in action. They may look very primitive - and so they are - but they are effective.

The track leads to Velliantatika square from where the lane to the right returns to the bus route [D]. **Ahead is the road to Fanariotatika,** to the right of a large white church facing the square. A lane behind the church leads under the arch of a flat walled campanile with two bells. It is worth exploring the little village before continuing along the lane to Fanariotatika.

Nearly all the hamlets in Paxos are named after the families that live there. The same families, generations ago, built the island's 63 churches, eg FANARIOTATIKA church (St Anayiri) was built by the FANARIOTIS family; MAKRATIKA church (Pantocrator "The Almighty") was built by COUNT MAKRIS; the BOGDANOS families built St Paraskevi at BOGDANATIKA, and so on.

Continuing towards Fanariotatika you will see pomegranate trees with fruit which ripens in October. If it is not the olive season you will notice black olive nets neatly rolled and stored in the trees.

Follow the track until it makes a sharp left hand bend and **a rough track leads straight on [E]. Follow this track past a church** on the right and soon you pass a right hand track which disappears towards a ruin in the olives **[F]**. It is possible to swim from the flat rocks in the bay far below by taking this track, although the path is vague.

For the headland keep ahead. The track ends in a walled glade and **a walled path** (Greek THROMAKI) **takes its place [G]. Follow this** through a stand of aromatic coniferous trees **and bear left where the path branches,** passing a stone building set into the wall on the right. The umbrella pine on the left can be seen from miles around. The walls end and the **path continues into a copse of Cypress trees** (Greek KIPAREESI). Suddenly **you emerge onto heathland** with panoramic views through 180° **[H]**. To the south over a hillside and valley you can see ANTIPAXOS, and KHIROS HEADLAND at Mousmouli (walk 16). To your right as you wander down the heathery promontory you have a view of five headlands. **You are near the edge of a sheer precipice which drops down to an inaccessible bay below.** To the north (below you on the right as you look over the precipice) are the gently shelving rocks (mentioned above) from which it is possible to swim. The low rocky headland of AGRILAS hides from view AVLAKI CREEK (walk 8) and OSTRIAS ESCARPMENT (walk 15) is above to the right. Vlachopoulatika village (walks 9 and 21) is hidden in the trees on the hillside above sheer cliffs, on the far side of the bay of Prasses. The headland further to the left (walk 23) is guarded by craggy ORTHOLITHOS stack. In the background is Point Pounda (walk 20) to the north of Achaii Bay. From this position you will gain an impression of the extent of the cliffs of Paxos' west coast and how totally inaccessible most of the coast is other than by boat.

There is not only the stunning scenery to enjoy from this headland: bird song, the buzz of insects in the heather and the gentle lapping of waves at the foot of the cliff add to the magic of the area. The tangy scent of sea mingles with the fragrant smell of juniper, cypress and broom. With chats and shrikes, flycatchers and larks to watch flying over the heathland, what better spot could you find for a picnic!

TO RETURN: By the same route, or Avlaki creek can be reached by zigzagging down the hillside from **[F]**, in which case you will return to the road by the lower path described in walk 8.

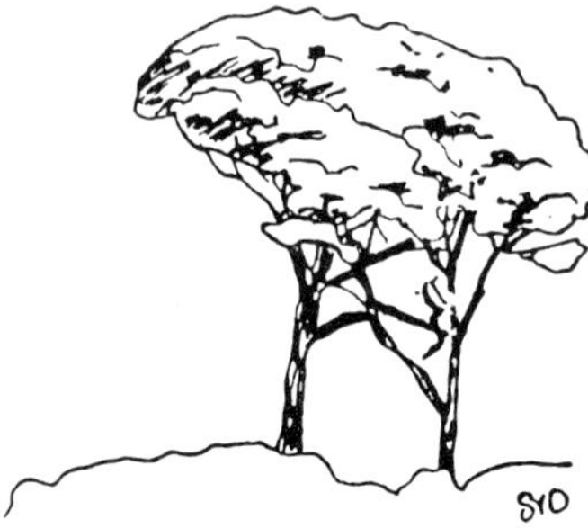

Umbrella Pines, St Nicholaos Island

23. HEADLAND VIEW NEAR ORTHOLITHOS 1 3/4 miles (2.8 km)

Made accessible by the construction of a road in 1988, the headland opposite Vlachopoulatika is now easily reached by lane and makes an enjoyable excursion.

From the same starting point as walks 2, 9 and 21.

STARTING POINT: **[h] The road junction for Vlachopoulatika, at the bus stop**, between Bogdanatika and Magazia.

Starting from the taverna at the roadside, take the concrete road **past the football pitch which is on the left [j]**. Family groups of goats can sometimes be seen wandering through the olives, their bells tinkling. If not hobbled, they frequently stand on their hind legs to reach the leaves of the trees. Kids in particular will jump up into the branches for a good view of their surroundings. The nanny goats are milked every day or two days, and the milk is used to make fetta cheese - an essential ingredient in many Greek meals, especially Greek Salad (HORRIATIKI, lit. 'from the village').

On your right you can see the tall baroque bell tower of St Charalambos (see walk 13). **Take a turning downhill [k] to the right** and hidden in the olives on the right you will see an attractive little church **[m]** and campanile set against the hillside. The road follows the flank of the cypress-clad hillside, passing a ruin on the right. A left-hand bend brings the sea into view.

At a fork [n] take the left hand bend downhill (the right hand lane rejoins the main road at ARVANITAKEIKA). **You reach a fork and turn** downhill to the **left [p]**. Continuing along the lane you have a view to your left of an endless shimmering blue sea.

Should you at any time be travelling at night along the main road (above you), pause, and you will be entranced by the unforgetable sight of the moon casting a path of silver light across a calm black sea, while fireflies flicker their mysterious greenish lights. The lonely hoot of a Scops Owl interupts the incessant chirring of cicadas (Greek TZEETZEEKAS) and the bird-like "peeep" of a gecko.

As you continue, a track joins your lane from below on the left and you reach a walled field on the right in which vines and fruit are grown **[q]**. The walls around vineyards are constructed so that a line of stones juts out just below the top, and heather is laid beneath the top stones. The walls serve primarily to keep out goats and sheep. They also afford some protection for the crops from the winds which are hot, dry and dusty during the summer.

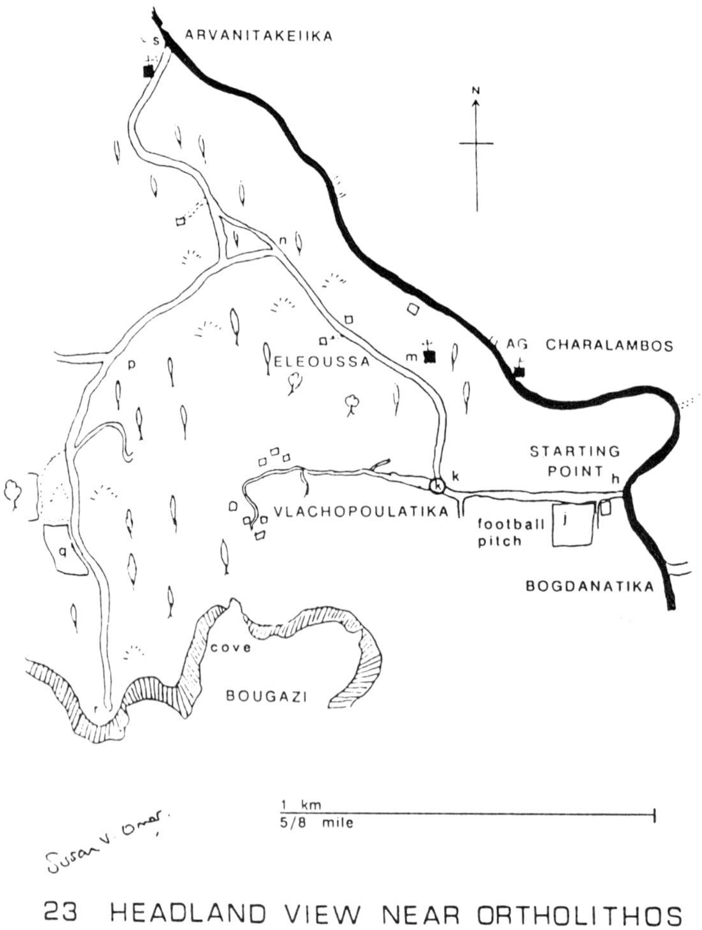

23 HEADLAND VIEW NEAR ORTHOLITHOS

A little further along the lane **you reach the end of the path** at a walled garden which connects to another of Paxos' vineyards **[r]**. You will see many examples of neglected terraced vineyards on the west coast: nowadays grape production is concentrated in Antipaxos which has a small output of very fine wine. From this headland, not far from Ortholithos (which is not in sight) you have a superb view to the south and west of mile upon mile of green-blue sea under a cloudless sky.

At the foot of a hillside below you is the remarkable blue creek reached by walk 9. This is one of the few places from which the little inlet can be seen. On the far hillside is Vlachopoulatika, and beyond is the Bay of Prasses bordered by inaccessible cliffed beaches. A lonely umbrella pine marks the top of Fanariotatika Headland (walk 22). In the distance Antipaxos and perhaps Cephalonia and Lefkada are visible.

<u>TO RETURN</u>: The uphill lane at [n] leads to Arvanitakeika (3/8 mile or 1.6 km) **[s]** from which you can join the start of walk 20 to Sts Apostoli, and **the bus also stops there. Alternatively you can return to your starting point.**

View southwards from Walk 23 showing "Pirates Cove" in foreground Fanariotatika Headland (walk 22) and Antipaxos (background)

The Shops of Paxos are full of surprises

Glossary

Many of the terms below are given in the hope that they will be adopted by the visitor, as they are particularly applicable to walking and exploring the countryside. Use of them, together with a phrase book, saves much uncertainty and a great deal of time while asking for directions and chatting to the local people, and naturally the Greeks will be delighted to hear you using even a few of their phrases.

Almighty, the	o Pantocrator	*ο Παντοκράτωρ*
apostles	apostoli	*απόστολοι*
beach	paraleea	*παραλία*
brackish water	glypha	*γλύφα*
bus	leoforeeo	*λεωφορείο*
butterfly	petaloutha	*πεταλούδα*
cape/headland	akrotiri	*ακρωτήρι*
carob tree	koutsoupia or haroopia	*κουτσουπία / χαρούπια*
catchment pit (oil)	katolavri	*κατωλάυρι*
cave / cavern	spillia	*σπηλιά*
cavity	trippa	*τρύπα*
church	eckliseea	*εκκλησία*
cicadas	tzeetzeekas	*τζίτζικας*
cliff	gremmos	*γκρεμός*
coffee	kafai	*καφέ*
coffee house	cafeneio(n)	*καφενείο(ν)*
Corfu	Kerkyra	*Κέρκυρα*
cove	ormos	*όρμος*
creek	kolpiskos	*κολπίσκος*
cypress tree	kipareesi	*κυπαρίσσι*
donkey	yitharos	*γάιδαρος*
footpath (see path)		
garden	keepos	*κήπος*
goat	katseeka	*κατσίκα*
great	megalo	*μεγάλο*
Greek salad	horriatiki	*χωριάτικη*
grinding wheel	litharo(s)	*λίθαρο(ς)*
grouse/partridge	perthika	*πέρδικα*
gypsy	yeeftos	*γύφτος*
headland/cape	akrotiri	*ακρωτήρι*
heather	reeki	*ρείκι*
heathland	reekia	*ρεικιά*
hedgehog	skantzoheeros	*σκαντζόχοιρος*

island	nisee	*νησί*
lemonade	lemonatha	*λεμονάδα*
lighthouse	pharos	*φάρος*
lookout post	vigla	*βίγλα*
mill (see windmill)		
myrtle	myrtia	*μυρτιά*
New Port	Neo Limani	Νέο Λιμάνι
olive (tree and fruit)	ellia	*εληά*
olive oil	elleeolathon, lathi	*ελαιόλαδον, λάδι*
olive press (see press)		
orangeade	portokolatha	*πορτοκαλάδα*
Pan Helenic Socialist Movement		Π.Α.Σ.Ο.Κ.
path	thromakos	*δρομάκος*
port	limani	*λιμάνι*
press (olive)	litrouvio	*λιτρουβιό*
road	thromos	*δρόμος*
Saint/Saints	Aghios/Aghiee	Αγιος/Αγιοι
scrubland	hammoklatha	*χαμόκλαδα*
sea	thalassa	*θάλασσα*
spindles (olive press)	athraktia	*αδράχτια*
square	plateea	*πλατεία*
stack (rock pillar in sea)	ortholithos	*ορθόλιθος*
stranger (guest)	xenos/xen(i)	*ξένος/ξενη*
stroll	volta	*βόλτα*
sun	ilios	*ήλιος*
tank/reservoir	sterna	*στέρνα*
tree	thendro	*δένδρο*
view	thaya	*θέα*
village	horrio	*χωριό*
Virgin Mary, Madonna	Panayia	Παναγία
well/spring	pigarthi	*πηγάδι*
wind (on Paxos esp.)	Maestro (N), and Scirocco (Tropical)	
windmill, mill	meelos	*μύλος*

SEASONS

Spring	Aneeksee	Ανοιξη
Summer	Kalokerri	Καλοκάιρι
Autumn	Ftheenoporron	Φθινόπωρον
Winter	Himona	Χειμώνας

DAYS OF THE WEEK

Sunday	Kiriakee	Κυριακή
Monday	Theftera	Δευτέρα
Tuesday	Triti	Τρίτη
Wednesday	Tetarti	Τετάρτη
Thursday	Pempti	Πέμπτη
Friday	Paraskevi	Παρασκευή
Saturday	Savato	Σάββατο

USEFUL PHRASES

yes / no	neh / ocki	*ναι / οχι*
please	parakalo	*παρακαλώ*
thankyou	efharisto	*ευχαριστώ*
good morning	kalimera	*καλημέρα*
good evening	kalispera	*καλησπέρα*
hello (singular/plural)	yia soo/ yia sas	*γειά σου /γειά σας*
goodbye (as hello) or	adeeo	*αντίο*
how are you?	ti kanees?/ti kanete?	*τι κάνεις ,/τι κάνετε;*
fine thanks	kalla efharisto	*καλά ευχαριστώ*
cheers	stin-y-yiassas	*στήν υγειά σας*
good appetite	kali orexi	*καλή όρεξη*
I am sorry	signomi	*συγγνώμη*
excuse me	mai seenkhoreetai	*με συγχωρείτε*
I don't understand	then katalaveno	*δεν καταλαβάινω*
I don't know	then ksero	*δεν ξέρω*
where is...?	poo eenai...?	*που έιναι...;*
left	aristera	*αριστερά*
right	theksyia	*δεξιά*
straight on	evtheea/ eesia	*ευθεία /ίσια*
have a good journey!	kalo taxithi	*καλό ταξίδι*

Acknowledgements

I would like to extend a broad "thank you" to the many Paxiots who have been tremendously helpful to me over the past two years, in particular Polyxeni Alimerioti and Yiorgia Makri.

I owe the entire production and management of this booklet to my cousin Moira Römer, who has put in countless hours of work and many visits to Paxos for this cause. To my husband Tarek and my parents Bryan and Patricia Picking I am grateful for much advice and encouragement.

Other grateful thanks to Diana Blake and David Römer for proof reading and constructive comments; for technical assistance Sandra Lodge of Gabletek Limited, Richard Chandler of Imaging Systems Limited, and Geoffrey Morgan of Sutton Griffin & Morgan.

Finally, I acknowledge the support of Corfu à la carte (villa holidays) of Stockcross, Newbury, with whom I was employed while on Paxos, and without whom I should never have discovered the island.

The author is always pleased to hear from readers. Your opinions and ideas for future editions of this book are most welcome. Please contact Susan Omar c/o Römer Designs, Trees, Cold Ash, Newbury, RG16 9HZ, England.